AN AUT

THE JOURNEY SO FAR

GILBERT EBHOTE EIGBOBO

THE JOURNEY SO FAR

AN AUTOBIOGRAPHY

By
GILBERT EBHOTE EIGBOBO

ParaMount Books
by : Kenzi

Most Paramount Titles
are also available at major online book retailers.
Copyright (c) 2018 Gilbert Eigbobo All rights reserved under International Copyright Law. Written permission must be secured from the publisher/author to reproduce, copy, or transmit any part of this book. Unless otherwise marked, all Scripture quotations are taken from the NIV/KJV, and the Scripture quotations noted NIV are taken from the HOLY BIBLE, NEW INTERNATIONAL VERSION®. Copyright © 1973, 1978, 1984 by International Bible Society. Used with permission. Scriptures noted KJV is from the King James Version of the Holy Bible. Used with permission.

ISBN -13: 978-1723308338

ISBN-10: 1723308331

Because of the dynamic nature of the Internet, any web addresses or links contained in this book may have changed since publication and may no longer be valid. Any people depicted in stock imagery provided by Think stock are models, and such images are being used for illustrative purposes only.

Certain stock imagery © Thinkstock.

Published in the United States of America by

Paramount Books by Kenzi. ®

Contact Paramount Books by Kenzi® for all your Publishing.

paramountdirector@yahoo.co.uk

orxtyn@yahoo.com

Table of Content

A Note to Readers.

Acknowledgments.

Dedication

Preface.

Prologue.

Foreword.

INTRODUCTION:

Who Am I?

The Daring Trip of Two Kid Brothers

Life in a Polygamous Home

Change of Name Instigated by my Father.

The illness and Transition of my Father

Annual Easter Family Reunion.

Benefits of my Father's Legacy

Selfish Perception about the Girl Child Education

The Art of Spinning & Weaving

Communal Life in my Village.

Chapter 1: 54

MY EARLY LIFE.

POWER OF KNOWLEDGE/EDUCATION

Chapter 2: 66

EARLY EDUCATION/PARENTAL CONTROL

MISSED OPPORTUNITIES

Chapter 3: 75

SEARCH FOR EMPLOYMENT

DECISION TO STUDY PITMAN'S SHORTHAND

Chapter 4: 81

SECURING MY FIRST EMPLOYMENT

TRAUMATIC LIFE EXPERIENCE IN LAGOS

RISE ABOVE MENIAL JOBS

ATTEMPT AT DISTRACTION BY FRIENDS

EMPLOYMENT AS A STENOGRAPHER

Chapter 5:   91

BREAKING NEW GROUND
REAPING THE FRUITS OF DILIGENCE
FIRST PROMOTION & CONVERSION
DEPARTMENTAL MERGER.
EXCEEDED EXPECTATION OF PROMOTION TO MANAGER.
CONVERSION TO BRANCH BANKING OPERATION.
IN-SERVICE TRAINING.
ACCELERATED PROMOTION/APPOINTMENT – MANAGER
PREPARING FOR RETIREMENT
AVOIDING UNNECESSARY EXPENDITURE
PLANNING FOR FINANCIAL SECURITY
REASONS FOR RETIREMENT

Chapter 6:   118

CHALLENGES OF MANAGING A COMMUNITY BANK
FIRST ARMED ROBBERY ATTACK
THE MENACE OF MEN OF THE UNDERWORLD
THE SECOND ARMED ATTACK
A THIRD ATTEMPT ATTACK – REPELLED
MIGRATION TO MICRO-FINANCE BANK
COMPUTERIZATION OF OPERATIONS

Chapter 7: 138
RAISING A FAMILY
CHALLENGE OF CHILDCARE/EVENTUAL MARRIAGE
UNIQUE WEDDING OF TWO DAUGHTERS.
TRAGIC HOME CALL OF CHRISTIANA
GRIEVING THE LOSS OF A LOVED ONE
ACKNOWLEDGING A KIND GESTURE
THE MYSTERIOUS WAYS OF GOD
RESISTING PRESSURE TO RE-MARRY
UNEXPECTED DEATH OF MY SON/TRIBUTE.
RESILIENCE WITH GOD'S HELP – A GRANDFATHER'S PRAYER

Chapter 8: 167
A TEST OF FAITH
THE TURNING POINT
FINDING THE WAY AND PEACE
PROFESSED OBLATE OF SAINT BENEDICT
THE LAUDABLE ACHIEVEMENTS OF CHRISTIANA
ERECTING THE GROTTO
WINNING SOULS FOR GOD'S KINGDOM
KNIGHTS & LADIES AUXILIARY OF SAINT JOHN INTERNATIONAL
VOLUNTARY WITHDRAWAL FROM RE-ELECTION

Chapter 9:   **183**

SOCIAL & SPORTING ACTIVITIES.

FORMATION OF FIRST BANK FOOTBALL CLUB "THE ELEPHANT BOYS"

CONCLUSION.

Chapter 10:   **190**

THE CHARACTERISTICS OF AGING PROCESS

AGING GRACEFULLY

PLANNING FOR THE FUTURE

GENESIS OF HIGH BLOOD PRESSURE DIAGNOSIS

LEAVING A LEGACY

EPILOGUE

FOREWORD

OBEHIAYE OGABI (DAUGHTER).

OSEGHALE (SON)" APPRECIATING MY WORTHY DADDY"

ISEDUA (DAUGHTER) "MY LITTLE JOURNEY IN DADDY'S

JOURNEY"

IFEOLUWA OGABI:(GRANDSON)

OLUWADAMILOLA OGABI: (GRANDSON) "MY GRANDPA"

-MAYOKUN OGABI(GRANDDAUGHTER): MY LOVING GRANDPA"

-TOBORE ERUVWETAGHWARE: GRANDDAUGHTER

-RUKEVWE ERUVWETAGHWARE: GRANDSON

-MARO ERUVWETAGHWARE: GRANDDAUGHTER

-BRUME ERUVWETAGHWARE.: GRANDDAUGHTER.

- OMONIGHO EIGBOBO (DAUGHTER)

- IGHEDOISE EIGBOBO (SON)

- ISIMENMEN OLABOOYE(GRANDSON)

- EHIMARE EIGBOBO   (GRANDSON)

- IKAEHO EIGBOBO   (GRANDDAUGHTER)

- EGHEOSE EIGBOBO (GRANDDAUGHTER)

A NOTE TO READERS:

If anyone needs a book that transcends the Autobiography of the Author to touch on real life issues, e.g. "Preparing early for Retirement;" "Peculiarities of aging process" & more, then you must read this book.

ACKNOWLEDGMENTS

As always, I have so many people to acknowledge for the writing of this book but as usual there is limited space.

To..... Joseph Ogabi, my son-in-law and his wife Obehiaye Ogabi (nee Eigbobo), for encouraging me to commence the writing of this book. It took a while for it to sink in, but my casual approach took a serious turn when they continually put me on the spot at the least opportunity with "grandpa's writing a book!" Thank you so much.

Members of The Redeemed Christian Church of God, King's Court Parish, Renton, WA. State, who constantly showed interest as they asked me "when will the book be ready & how's your book coming on?"

My Grand kids, Daniel, David and Abigail Ogabi who did not get tired of asking me, "Grandpa, are you still writing your book, when shall we get to read it?"

All my lovely kids who showed excitement that at last daddy's writing his autobiography.

The publisher, Pastor Austin Edeki and all others too numerous to mention who in one way or the other contributed to the eventual completion of this book; I do not take their efforts for granted. Their constant reminders helped to keep me on my toes and provided the impetus I needed to complete this book. All their contributions are appreciated.

Gil Eigbobo.

DEDICATION

I dedicate this book First and foremost to The Almighty God for His enablement for me to tell my story. Without life, good health and peace of mind, which He always gives me, writing this book would not have been a reality. Lord, I thank you.

 The memory of my late wife Christiana, who transited at the age of fifty-two; she led me to know God at my age sixty and my mother at age ninety in a remarkable way and thus paved the way for our salvation. Together we had toiled but, to the Glory of God, her sun set at noon, after a life of fulfilment. She was a guardian Angel sent by God and once her work was done, God called her home. Christiana continues to live in my heart.

The memory of my late son Gregory, who joined his mother at the bosom of The Lord in October 2017 at the age of almost forty-eight. "Son, my heart still bleeds." Young, but he achieved; he was a very important person in my life whose sun also set at noon. In his short life span, he showed me true love of a son. I give Glory to God and I respect His Will; Greg continues to live in my heart.

May the gentle souls of Christiana, Gregory, and the souls of all the faithful departed through the mercy of God continue to rest in peace. Amen.

Gil. Eigbobo.

PREFACE

Everyone has a story; this is mine.

"Daddy (as he fondly calls me), if you ask me, I think that you should write a book."- Joseph, my son-in-law continually said to me.

*I had misgivings at the beginning about starting to write my maiden book at nearly eighty-two years of age and I hesitated; but the inclination to do so caught my fancy after I had read books authored by men and women my age and even older; then the urge to tell my story began to grow stronger. Not having thought about writing a book previously, and this being my first one, I was initially bereft of ideas on how to start, where to start from and what to write about. Then gradually, "**Everyone has a story**," began to ring a bell in my ears.*

*"Why don't I tell my own story now while I have the time to do so?" I asked myself. "No mortal knows what tomorrow holds." By divine inspiration I eventually came up with the desire to share my memoirs, and like the man next door, because I had literally been on a journey since the day of my birth, the title "**The Journey So Far**" registered an impression on my mind. I find this title to be apt since the book largely contains a detailed account of virtually all aspects of my life that I can remember almost from cradle, through puberty and maturity, to aging. All the stories I tell in this book are true accounts of events that took place at one stage or another of my life thus far.*

PROLOGUE

The cultural and educational background of families of the two individuals who came together to give me life was coincidentally similar. By coincidence, both were born into polygamous homes, and nobody in both families had benefitted from any formal education before my birth. My paternal uncle, Wallace and my maternal uncle, Lawrence were the first beneficiaries of any formal education in the two families, and they both started elementary school at different times after I was born.

I believe that my father's decision to send me and all my brothers to school, even when he could not conveniently afford the cost, must have stemmed from his enlightened outlook to make up for his own unfulfilled dream to go to school.

Now, sit back - read on.

FOREWORD.

I am extremely proud of my Father in-law for this great accomplishment. His dedication and commitment to turn what was just a dream into a reality is quite commendable. Once he shook off the initial lethargy and he decided to put pen to paper, the story of his life as told in this book continued to flow and there was no stopping him. That this book was ready for publishing in less than twelve months from the commencement date is a testimony to the author's retentive memory at his age in putting together events spanning over eight-two years!

One of the greatest tragedies of life is to live and leave without leaving behind for generations to come, not just one's story but a legacy. This, no doubt, is a great legacy not only to the descendants or family members of Gilbert Eigbobo, but to as many who seek to reach their goals in life no matter where they are starting from.

The writings in this book are not just stories to be enjoyed although the reader will find most of them exciting. They contain life's lessons over challenges, acts of determination and persistence demonstrated through which the author has made his impact in the lives of his children, immediate and extended family as well as his friends and co-workers.

"Wisdom is with the aged and understanding in length of days" **Job 12: 12.**

This is very true when you make Christ the focus of your life. Mr. Gilbert Eigbobo has put into writing the wisdom & understanding he had gained over several decades.

Joseph Olusola Ogabi.

The Dad that I Know

One of my earliest memories of my dad as a little girl is of the times when he would come home from work during his lunch break to cook lunch for my younger siblings and I, and then return to work. My mom was attending hairdressing & Cosmetology school at that time, and my older siblings were at school. One of the things I have always appreciated the most about my dad is his devotion to family, and how that translated into him spending time with us. This early memory I have of him is one of many tangible examples of that devotion. Often on Saturday mornings while my siblings and I were busy with weekend chores or cooking breakfast with my mom, he would have music playing on his record player. Some of his favorite songs were those of Jim Reeves and Boney M, and as a result, he had several of their albums, and my siblings and I became familiar with many of their songs. At some point on those Saturday mornings he would start to dance to the music in the living room. Something about watching him dance and show off his ballroom dance skills just made us laugh a lot. Eventually, some or all of us would join in the dance with him, either as his dance partner or in our own freestyle dancing.

Many times, on weekends, he would take us driving in his car around town with no specific destination in mind. I realize now that he probably had a destination in mind on some of those occasions, but he just did not let us in on it. On some of those occasions, we would end up at the home of one of our friends or relatives, and other times we would end up at the beach in Lagos. We would play at the beach till late in the evening, and then get something to eat on our way home. Another frequent fun occurrence was when we would all sit on mats on the floor in front of our apartment at night, while my dad and mom told us folktales (usually involved the tortoise, hare or lion) or stories about their own childhood. Both my parents were strict, so having these regular times to just hang out with them provided a good balance.

When I think about my childhood, and especially now that I have children of my own, I feel that much is required of me as a parent, because "Unto whom much is given, much is required". My dad like any other dad is not perfect, but I know that my siblings and I were given much in terms of quality time with parents, who consciously made sacrifices and chose to invest in their children (and some not their own biological children). I am grateful for that.

Obehiaye Ogabi.

Appreciating my Worthy Dad.

Oseghale is my name but daddy fondly calls me "Osy" for short. I am the sixth of eight children of the Gilbert Eigbobo family. First, I want to appreciate God for what He has used my dad to do in the lives of his children and grandchildren. My dad has always been there for us and right now am short of words good enough to describe his limitless love and affection not only for us his kids but also all who have crossed his path. This book has given us the opportunity to have a fuller insight into how much he toiled and persevered, the result of which has made life worth living for us, yet he did not spare any pains to give us a good life. This book has revealed that he is a self-made man. I especially thank God for the strength that He allowed to flow through my dad, and as I read this wonderful piece of work, I imagined the tears he may have been fighting back as he wrote about our late sweet mother, his amiable wife and confidant. May God bless her gentle soul.

I could recall a time in Lagos when Obehiaye (my elder sister) had an encounter with the presence of God; the day she revealed it was another episode in our house. But in all these we see God's hand gently and subtly enter our family with His love and mercy, directing all our paths, which we work hard daily to perfect, as He gives us the zeal to serve Him more fervently.

I appreciate that my dad may have tried to summarize this book and events that started from that humble beginning and which culminated to a success story. His example has empowered and encouraged all of us that life can start at any level, no matter how demeaning it may look, but with diligence and dedication to the goals we set for ourselves, things can always get better. Undoubtedly, the transition of my big brother and friend, Gregory Omohomioria Eigbobo (God bless his soul) has created a big vacuum in our family which only God Himself can fill. My brother and I did have our times of differences though, which is normal, but I loved him very much. One thing I am grateful to dad and mum for today is their admonition to always respect our elders (which I will always remember) and which has helped me a lot, particularly in my working environment now. May the souls of Mummy, big brother Greg and the souls of all the faithful departed through the mercy of God rest in peace.

I want to take this opportunity to say "THANK YOU DADDY" for the life and upbringing he and mummy gave to us all their children while we were growing up. If there is any regret I have now, it is that mummy is not here to be by daddy's side to witness the goodness of God in the lives of her children and grandchildren here in Nigeria, the United States and the United Kingdom. We have been empowered by the lessons we have learnt from my dad's ideals of moral uprightness and wish to assure him that we will do our best to ensure that our children are brought up in a similar affectionate loving environment we had growing up. All those repeated weekend visits to places of interest, particularly Federal Palace Hotel where dad would let us play around before finally settling down to enjoy their Club Sandwich. I cannot forget the many picnics we enjoyed at the Bar Beach and Ikoyi Park.

Oseghale George Eigbobo

"My little journey in daddy's journey." _Isy.

My name is Isedua Georgina Eruvwetaghware (Née Eigbobo), popularly called "Isy" by everyone. Like most of us, the only few times I was called by my full name "Isedua" were whenever I was in trouble with my mother (God bless her soul). Growing up as the youngest daughter (not the youngest child though), in a powerful mix of 8 children was an amazing experience worth sharing. Sometimes, I wonder if my father, Gilbert Eigbobo, the author of this book, realized how much his strong and positive fatherly role impacted us his children.

Let me quickly jump in on one of my favorite experiences growing up. I remember very clearly how my father never allowed one single weekend to go to waste. When he was not taking us to the then popular Bar beach in Lagos Island, Nigeria, it was Federal Palace Hotel; Hmmmn!). Anyways, for us, it was such a joy to just run around these places with my dad as our personal tour guide. To us (I believe I speak for my siblings too here), it seemed as if my father knew something about everything. And then, we would crown the day with sitting down by the ocean front to some club sandwich while enjoying the view of ships either sailing or just anchored in. (I can almost still taste it now). When I think about it, I realize my father did not necessarily have all the money in the world to lavish on us, but he surely made every moment of my childhood count. We would always return home and later to school bragging to friends about the wonderful weekend experience with my dad. We were obviously the envy of our friends to have such a "cool Dad".

How many can I count? Even in the little everyday things that ordinarily did not mean much, my father always found a way to put a little excitement into it. Back then, in our 3-bedroom apartment on Oredola Isalemole close, off Fola Agoro Street, Lagos, Nigeria, where I mostly grew up, every one of our Neighbors even knew the peculiar honk of my father's car like a song (pompom, pompom Baba Osi). As soon as the first person heard that, we would all dash out to meet my father in the parking lot. You would think he was returning from a journey to a far country. The beauty of this was that sometimes, he really was returning from a far journey, but most times he was just returning from a normal day's hard work. Our neighbors' children always rallied round too like it was their father returning. Well, the reason was simple: my father never returned home with an empty trunk or car, and so there was always some "goodie" he would give them and say, "give this to your mother or father". Sometimes, it was something as simple as a tuber of yam. It kind of felt like having Father Christmas for a dad, but in retrospect, my father was not the wealthiest guy around, he just knew how to share whatever little God had blessed him with. What a lesson in giving, as well as nurturing relationships with neighbors.

I could go on and on, but this is not my book. It's my father's. Oh! I must add this too! I wonder if this meant as much to my father as it does to me; Sometimes, we weren't sure where we were going, but my father would get my siblings and myself in the car, and we would just go on rides with him

playing his best tunes in the car "cassette player". I still remember the words of one of the all-time favorite songs:
"I got a letter on Monday, but I couldn't reply, I got another on Tuesday, but I couldn't write, because writing a little letter wouldn't say everything that I have got in my mind to say.... come home, you better come home, come home, you better come home."

I still don't remember what the name of the artist of that song was, but in my mind, I like to think that those were songs my father may have sung to my mother, Christiana Ejimiagbon Eigbobo (of blessed memory) to continually woo and keep her in his loving heart. It was beautiful to later find out that my father had been a ballroom dance instructor and he told us he had tried to teach my mother the dance steps.

Growing up with my father was truly fun, with a balance though. As cool as he was, you never wanted to do something wrong or get on his bad side. That stern look from him sometimes made u feel like "please give me a whooping right now rather than this stare before I pee in my pants".

Oh! Let me quickly add also, one of my favorite Saturday morning moments. By this time though, we had moved from Lagos, in the southern part of Nigeria, to Irrua, Edo state, (formerly part of Western Nigeria.) My father would wake us up to the fresh aroma of roasted yellow yam. That meant that he was already awake before everybody, long enough to make fire outside and roast yams to cooked perfection. He then sent each of my siblings to bring the rest of the ingredients like fresh red palm oil, salt, and pepper, and everyone would dig in and eat hot pre-breakfast out of the same plate! How I miss those even now!

I have watched my father groom every young man that ever came his way with whatever piece of knowledge or experience he could impact. It didn't matter if they were directly related to him or not, he had something tangible to impact. From his brothers, nephews, or even a stranger or younger colleague, to his sons-in-laws (my darling husband, Apst Ese Erus included), my father found some virtue or knowledge or wisdom to impart in making/investing money, and even patterning a responsible life generally. He treated even his drivers with dignity and respect!

His grandchildren, our children (-Tobore, -Rukevwe, -Maro, and Brume) would often say with great excitement, "Grandpa is so cool, he knows a lot about everything!"

On this note, I would like to conclude with a birthday post I sent on Facebook a couple of years ago on my daddy's eightieth.

"Today daddy (Gil Eigbobo), I have u on my mind, and truly I can't help thanking God so much for giving u such a good life. Honestly, there aren't very many at 80 years old that look as good as u do. Watching you evolve and transform from grace and glory to grace and glory, and still u have not lost ur swag! Thank u for a very beautiful childhood u gave us all (and u're still giving your grandchildren). Those memories are highly treasured! There's never a dull moment around u!

Pls celebrate this "cool guy" that has refused to get old as

Jehovah continues to renew his youth. A prayer will do just fine.

Happy 80th daddy!

I could go on and on. Just couldn't let this day go by without sharing these thoughts today. We All love u!"

Thank you, daddy, for giving me ALL this space in your book. At almost 82 years old, you still got ur swag! Rock on Daddy!

Isedua Erus.

Grandpa

For as long as I could remember, nothing else on this planet could symbolize the elderly acting as young as my grandfather. Gilbert Eigbobo at times played more like a child than me and my siblings did. His energetic presence was always a pleasure to be enveloped. One could evidently understand our season of partial distress when our generous grandfather travelled to Atlanta, Georgia when we were quite young. His stay endured for a couple of months, which at the time passed like a couple of years.

One thing that our grandpa frequently did when we were young, was present us with "surprise." To be straight forward, what we referred to as surprise was simply a mint in the shape of a lifesaver. It was always one of the things my siblings and I looked forward to the most. "Surprise" would make a bad day appear like a new adventure.

From my point of view, when I was young, we had two moms in our family. There was the young one, and the old one. It is an easy guess to figure out that grandpa was the older one. Grandpa would be the one to take care of us when our parents were gone, and at times he would cook for us as well. For a majority of the time, grandpa was the one who would transport us to and from school. Grandpa was a firm rock that could only get stronger. At times he was the only person I wanted to be with. Whether he was taking us on a walk, or to the park for soccer, every day was a new lesson to make somebody's life better. That is why I completely love my grandpa.

Daniel Ogabi

My Grandpa.

One of my earliest memories of Grandpa was when he had come back from Nigeria. It was a long time ago, but I vaguely remember Grandpa going back and forth from his home-country to the US. Finally, he settled here, content with his choice. My life would be very different if he had stayed in Nigeria. It kind of makes me feel special, that of all the children he chose to stay with, it was my mom. Grandpa has had a huge impact on this family, and it has often, I feel, been taken for granted.

Without Grandpa, my parents would probably have lost a lot of money and might not have been able to pursue their careers. When me and my siblings were going into school, and my parents had to work, Grandpa was there, at home, taking care of us. When my Mom had to go to different states and even different countries to complete her schooling, Grandpa was there, making sure that my Dad wasn't overwhelmed by us three children. When my Dad got promoted but had to work night shift for an extensive period, Grandpa was in the house, making sure that we didn't bother my Mom when she was studying or at work. For as long as I could remember, my Grandpa was there, when my parents either had work, school, or various programs to go to. Grandpa was almost always at home, making sure that there was an adult at home. If not for Grandpa, our family wouldn't have gotten half as far as we are now.

Grandpa has always been that guy to be active, still be involved in things. He goes for groceries occasionally, when

my parents are busy. He sometimes gives us treats if we go along with him. Whenever he is asked about his age and he answers, everyone always says,
"Eighty! You don't look eighty. Wow!"
He certainly doesn't act eighty either. Occasionally, when we all go out together to play tennis, Grandpa is right there with us. People always say, "Once you've gotten to a certain age, there's really nothing that you can do." That's certainly not the case with Grandpa. I'm not really an expert on other elderly people, since Grandpa is the only one I really know, but I'm pretty sure that he is active for his age.
Grandpa is someone that is generally a fun person to be around. He makes you laugh and is someone that really flourishes in his golden age. He's not just our Grandpa though. Almost all our friends regard him as Grandpa and is someone that everyone respects and loves. He's more helpful than he cares to admit. When he's gone, there will be a significant hole in our family. I know that this may be a bit of a cliché, but I really do believe that he really is the best grandfather in the world.

David Ogabi.

My Loving Grandpa.

If everything and everyone in my life is a part of me then without my grandpa a huge chunk of me would be missing. I can only but the most imagine what my life would be like, either my mom would have to drop out of school or my dad might have to quit his job. The most logical and convenient solution would have been to find a babysitter (to tell the truth I have always wanted to know what it was like to have one) but anyway, why pay a stranger you found on the phone when your grandpa can take care of you and your siblings and get this - and it's for free!

Now that's an offer our parents probably can't resist! At first, I didn't realize it but now as I'm typing this, I do. My grandpa was literally always there for me when he could make it, of course. But when I really take the time to stop and think about all he has done for me I feel like I'm taking him for granted so I stop whatever I'm doing and take the time to pray to God and thank Him for my grandpa's life and hope he has many more years of it to come.

Abigail Ogabi.

For Grandpa's Book.

My grandpa is one of the most wonderful people I know. He is kind, generous and has a beautiful personality. I always look forward to his visits, like the last one when he came to surprise us at the park. All of us were so excited and jumped up to go give him a hug. I love my grandpa so much and cannot wait to read this book.

-*Tobore Eruvwetaghware*

About My Grandpa.

My Grandpa is sweet, funny, kind and has a great sense of humor. For instance, when he came for our church anniversary I asked him a question and he made it into a story about my mom when she was young. It went something like this: They were going to church a-n-d - well I can't remember more.

My Grandpa can make a story out of anything. He is so caring that he even stayed two days extra with my family and just for me – how caring! If I had to describe my grandpa I would say everything good, that is how awesome he is. My grandpa is a great cook. Once he made okra soup and it looked mouthwatering and tasted better than it looked.

-*Maro Eruvwetaghware*.

For Grandpa's Book

Anybody that knows my grandpa should know this. If I had to describe grandpa, I would say he's selfless, kind and outstanding. My grandpa loves and knows all his grandkids. He knows the year, day and month that each of his grand children was born. My grandpa is so caring he used his time to take me to Dollar Tree just, so I could buy chips, gum and a mechanical pencil. In conclusion, my grandpa is a spectacular, outstanding, selfless and wonderful man.

Rukevwe Eruvwetaghware

I love My Grandpa.

-Brume Eruvwetaghware.

My Daddy.my Daddy.

Daddy has always been a strong presence all through my life. Lovingly strict to ensure we the children never went astray growing up and he would still make time to play and joke.
I remember those Saturdays when before we woke up daddy had already roasted yam with firewood for breakfast; those were always lovely days when we ate breakfast before morning chores. There were the dancing days when he

played Jim Reeves music, and everyone danced in our own style. The only times we ate dinner without daddy was when he travelled because he would always come home from work in time for dinner with the family.

Even when daddy would not go to mass he ensured our spiritual training was never lacking; he was at every spiritual outing and you had no reason to miss catechism class as he would ask questions when you came back from class. Most Sundays we had outings which we always looked forward to; he always had something fun planned and the day always ended with dinner at a fabulous place.

Daddy would often take us for a walk; he was full of energy. I remember one evening we went for a walk with him from our Fola Agoro Street, Abule Ijesha, Lagos to uncle Mike's house at Ojuelegba, Surulere, which was quite a distance, but we didn't notice how far we had walked. Uncle Mike is daddy's younger brother; he didn't believe we walked to his house until he escorted us to the bus stop and he did not see the car; we still walked back home too. My dad has always been our strong pillar of support, I love him and am super proud of him.

Eigbobo, Gillian Omonigho.

About My Dad.

What can be said about a father? Some people believe that being a biological parent is sufficient for a man to be called a father, but I believe they are wrong. What a man does after a child is born is what really matters, the sacrifices made, dreams and personal desires forgone, the pains & anxieties endured for the sake of one's children are what I believe entitles one to be called a FATHER.

Gilbert Eigbobo, the author of this book is such a father. His life has been and is still a source of inspiration not only to his children but also to everyone who has encountered him. Although growing up I used to perceive some of his admonitions and rules as being harsh and unfair at that time, as most kids often do, I have come to appreciate and value them immensely now that I am a father myself. My dad has been and continues to be a light shining brightly on life's path for us his children to see our way, and I hope I can be as good a father as he has been to us all. That is why we all love him dearly.

Ighedoise Godfrey Eigbobo.

I was excited when my grandpa called to tell me he was writing his autobiography and he wanted to know if I'd like to say something in the book. He called again to tell me "it must be brief". "How do I write something 'brief' about this man I have come to know throughout my twenty-nine years of existence?" I wondered. Do I start from the excitement that filled the air whenever I was told that we would be spending the holidays with him, or living in my teenage years during which he taught me how to be independent, morally upright and financially responsible?

I remember when I was much younger, maybe seventeen, I was given some money and I felt like a king. He waited for me to squander the money; then he woke me up one morning and said to me "Gbenga, before I get back from work I want you to prepare a list of how you spent that money." Oh my God, that was not a good week for me. That is one of the many things I learnt from my grandpa – how to be financially responsible! It is not the big moments in life that matter most, though those are important, but it is the small things we do that count; like fixing something around the house without being asked or offering a kind word when needed. Grandpa has been a source of motivation to me, and I was pleased to know that he is writing his autobiography because I know that many people will benefit from his wisdom. He is kind and has always been supportive.

I just want to say, "thank you" to grandpa for all that he instilled in me and for all the memories and lessons he gave

me. I have a lot of positive things to tell my children and will always remember grandpa with appreciation.
Isimenmen Olugbenga Olabooye.

Ehimare is my name but grandpa calls me Mare. Remembering my childhood days with grandpa is fun that never escapes my memory. Living alone with him as a little child was always fun. I remember that everywhere grandpa went I was always with him; whenever he travelled to Lagos or Akure in Nigeria he always took me along, he never left me behind. I was like a little soldier or bodyguard to him. I have missed grandpa since the day he travelled to the United States of America. One thing I like about my him is that he is a good cook. Most times I wonder if all his male children learnt from him how to cook because they all cook like grandpa. I will always remain grateful to my grandpa because he taught me how to respect elderly people always. I really benefitted from his moral teachings from which I will never depart.
I am inspired by the book grandpa is writing and I am sure it will touch the lives of many of his readers positively. I pray that God will continue to grant him abundant blessings, strength and long life in good health.
Ehimare Samuel Eigbobo.

Christina is my name, but my grandpa calls me Ikaeho, the name that he gave to me. My grandpa is a smart and intelligent man. He is kind loving and caring; when I was a little girl he gave me a nickname that I love so much, "dimples". He always helps me whenever I need his help. I have always known him to be gentle, nice and he has always been there for me. I love him so much because of the pampering and care he shows to me even though he is now very far away from me. I have missed my grandpa since he travelled to America. I always pray to God to bring him back to me.

Ikaeho Christina Eigbobo.

My name is Athalia Egheose (God's time), and Gilbert Eigbobo is my grandpa. I have not met him, but my daddy told me that his favorite food is pounded yam and black soup. I love my grandpa so much with all my heart, I always talk with him and I even see him on the telephone. His hair is white, and he is sweet and cute. I miss him so much.

Egheose Athalia Eigbobo.

INTRODUCTION
Who Am I?

I was born on May 9, 1936 in Ubiaja town which was the divisional headquarter of Ishan Division in Benin Province, (now Esan South East Local Government Area of Edo State) in the Southern part of Nigeria, to the family of Pa Sadoh Oghuma Eigbobo and Madam Theresa Omoiholo Eigbobo (nee Omodiagbe). Ubiaja was my birthplace but both of my parents hailed from Irrua Town also in Ishan Division of Benin Province (now Esan Central Local Government Area of Edo State), of Nigeria. My father's birth place, Idumebo, and my mother's Ikekogbe, are about one and half miles apart.

While growing up, I learned that my paternal and maternal grandfathers, were good friends. They were also both hunters who undertook their hunting escapades together often. When my paternal grandfather learnt of the birth of my mother, he immediately asked for her hand in marriage to his eldest son, Sadoh, my father, as was common then in my clime. She was then betrothed to him; it was as simple as that. Both my father and my mother were minors at the time and they grew up to accept the fact that they would become husband and wife. When they were of age, the marriage was formalized, and not only did it produce seven children, it lasted till death did them part.

I can say with some level of certainty that ninety-nine percent of such match-making, if it still exists anywhere today, would end up hitting the rock once the children involved grow up; no child today wants to have a spouse chosen by a parent even if the child believes that the spouse would be the best among his/her suitors! Every child now prefers to find a spouse by him/herself and to be the one to introduce the spouse to the parents.

Despite the fruitfulness of that marriage, my father still went ahead to marry two more wives and thus presided over a polygamous home. I am the fourth of eleven children to my father and the third of seven to my mother in a unique polygamous home. Unique because, unlike most polygamous homes where children got attached more to their mothers than their fathers and sometimes alienated their half-siblings, ours was one in which all the children were united under our father. He had absolute unifying control over the affairs of his children.

I grew up to know that my father was an only surviving son to his mother in my grandfather's home. That informed his desire to give birth to many children. Happily, he was blessed with five boys and six girls, among whom I am one, and by God's Grace, we all survived him. His maternal siblings, Oribhabor, Ajogbor and Omoye, with whom he had close affinity were born into a separate family at the neighboring town of Ekpoma in Esan West Local Government Area of Edo State in Nigeria. We, his children were also close to them, particularly those of their own children who were within our age groups.

We did not know the basis of our relationship as children and did not even bother to find out then. We just knew that we were related. Often, we went to spend our long holidays with the young Oribhabors and we helped with their farm work just as they also periodically came to help with ours. Joseph, the eldest son of Ajogbor was educated and worked as a court clerk. My half-brother John, and I occasionally went to spend Christmas holidays wherever he was transferred to in Ishan Division largely because we knew we would get a chance to play with two of his younger brothers, John and Gabriel, who lived with him and were within our age group. We knew also that we would get to eat rice and meat at Christmas, which, in my clime in those days were among consumable commodities only within the reach of the affluent families at times other than festive periods. We walked most of the time because of the dearth of commercial vehicular movement at that time, and my father would not spare us the use of his bicycle because he had to go to work while we went to spend our holidays.

The Daring Trip of Two Kid Brothers.

One such trip worthy of special mention took place in 1948. I was a few months shy of twelve years of age and John was almost thirteen. Our Cousin, Joseph was based at Ogwa, Ishan Division of Benin Province in Southern Nigeria, a town we were to know later was about eighteen miles away. As my father often did, he had permitted us to go and spend the Christmas and New Year holidays with his Nephew, Joseph and he gave us money for transportation. We had neither been to Ogwa before nor did we know the road to the town. We did not even know how far away from Irrua Ogwa was at the time. While my father went to work, my half-brother John, and I set out early on a December morning on the week of Christmas to wait at Usugbenu road intersection.

Apart from very scanty personal cars, the only other vehicles that plied that road through Igueben to Agbor at that time were rickety trucks which infrequently conveyed logs of timber to Agbor. The truck drivers did not have any scheduled movement to follow and we did not have any idea of their take-off points. It was possible to see one or more trucks in any one day and it was also possible to not see any in one week. Finding one was therefore a 'chance card.' We waited all morning and not one truck came by on that day. It was turning out to not be our lucky day for such a journey and anxiety set in.

Just about midmorning, under the dry harmattan December sun, we sighted our father at a distance returning from work and we hid ourselves from his view. We believed that if he saw us still waiting at that time of the day, he might admonish us to return to the house and the opportunity to travel to Ogwa that Christmas might be lost. But we were already in the mood for travelling and were willing to do anything to not be stopped!

Once our father had passed without seeing us, John and I decided to set off on foot in the vain hope that we could see one truck to pick us up along the road to Igueben town, which we knew was ten miles away. Alas! we did not see even one truck up to the time we arrived at Igueben. We did not know anywhere or anybody in Igueben town and we were already tired, hungry and worn out after walking the long lonely untarred road on our bare feet. Having arrived at Igueben, we found out that we were already midway between our home and our destination.

Confused, tired and unsure how many more miles we had to walk to Ogwa, we pondered on whether to proceed or return home; either way, it was a long journey. Expectedly, we both agreed to continue the journey to Ogwa town. We then walked - and sometimes jogged - and soon we arrived at another road intersection between Igueben and Ebele town. We saw an isolated wooden signpost in the middle of nowhere with the inscription "Ogwa three miles," pointing to our right. At that time, our clothes wet from sweat, it was almost dusk and, considering that we were tired after already walking about fifteen miles, the three miles appeared to us very long and seemingly unachievable.

I took a deep breath, looked at my brother and the lonely narrow untarred road to Ogwa; I wished we were already at the end of our journey and for me, it was like starting all over again. We walked the three miles distance without seeing a single house or even any human being; just two of us frightened little kids walking such a lonely road at that time of the day. The three miles journey turned out to be all through a forest and as we continued, the sounds coming from the huge tall trees were frightful.

For the first time throughout the journey, our joyous expectation which had been our strength gave way to fear and anxiety when twice we saw animals we could not recognize jump across the narrow road ahead of us. We thought about the likely danger we were facing, and for once, we feared for our lives.

"Wild animals could inhabit this thick forest, you know." I said to my brother, John.

"Maybe, but we have no choice now but to move on?" he replied tersely. I guessed he was only trying to be strong!

Those early years of my life were devoid of what today are highway robberies, kidnappings, ritual killings or other forms of child abuses prevalent now in the society. There were no enemies to fear and everybody was more of his brother's keeper, especially where children needed help. So, our fears were not about possible hurt by humans but wild animals.

There was no electricity in Ishan then but luckily for us it was full moon and it shone brightly. It was nearly bed time when we arrived at our destination and finding someone to lead us to the house of the only court clerk in a small town like Ogwa was not difficult. Apparently, our potential hosts could not be informed in advance that we were on our way because of the dearth of easy means of communication at that time; so, they were not expecting us. When we knocked at their door, they were very surprised to see us, but they received us well, albeit with much sympathy when they knew that we walked all that long distance.

When my brother and I looked at our fingers, each was almost twice as big as its normal size and we were told it was because of the flow of blood arising from swinging them all through the eighteen miles journey almost non-stop! As dinner was being fixed for us that night we slept off on the sofa and did not wake up till the following morning. They understandably allowed us to sleep. We had a good one and our fingers had returned to their normal sizes when we woke up the following morning. Like the children that we were, we had forgotten about our previous day's ordeal and we accompanied John and Gabriel to fetch water from the stream. We enjoyed the rest of our time at Christmas and the New Year celebration.

All too soon, it was time to return home. The only means of transportation our cousin Joseph possessed was a Raleigh bicycle. Anxiety gripped John and I, and the fun we had at

Christmas and New Year celebrations vanished from our minds in a hurry. "How do we go back to Irrua? Are we still going to walk back?" We asked ourselves in hushed tones. Unknown to us, our cousin had arranged with his friend in the town who owned a kit car, (now known as pick-up truck) and he kindly dropped us off at home. Ironically, out of fear of the repercussion should our parents know that we walked to Ogwa, we did not disclose to anyone back home how we travelled!

LIFE IN A POLYGAMOUS HOME

Unfortunately, ours was one polygamous home in which there was no love lost between my father's wives due to the usual unhealthy rivalry which leads to cold war in most polygamous homes. My father told me it was his desire that they lived happily together, but he said he could not totally achieve that, try as he did. Therefore, as a panacea for unity among all his children, my father decided to focus less on his wives' acrimony and more on ensuring that none of them could significantly play any selfish dominant role in the upbringing of her own children to the exclusion of the other children.

My father succeeded in inculcating in us the spirit of oneness, such that no child was alienated from another one for reason of being born by another woman. Apart from my eldest brother, Sunday, who lived briefly with my maternal grandparents, all the eleven of us were raised in our home. That helped to foster a strong and understanding family unity among the children.

My father was a very strong-willed man, full of wits. Despite the acrimony among his wives, he made sure that we the children were so united under him that it was difficult for any visitor to our house to identify who was the mother of which child because of the way we interacted with each other. That close family bond remained so to the day my father joined his ancestors in September of 1975.

CHANGE OF NAME INSTIGATED BY MY FATHER.

Growing up, I answered the last name 'Sadoh,' which was my father's first name, and even went through elementary school answering that name. It was common knowledge in my community that all through past generations, most men, perhaps selfishly, did not want their own names to be forgotten after their death, particularly if they gave birth to male children who survived them. But my father looked at life differently because of his enlightened outlook. In 1961, it was he himself, who in his wisdom advised all his male, and unmarried female children, to change our last name from Sadoh (his first name) to Eigbobo which was our grandfather's first name. According to him, Eigbobo was more easily identifiable than Sadoh to any Ishan person wherever we might meet one anywhere we went to in the world.

That necessitated a formal change of my last name in 1961 from Sadoh, to Eigbobo which, to this day has become adopted as the family name by all my father's male and unmarried female children. All my male siblings' children and those of my own male and unmarried female kids also automatically adopted Eigbobo as their last name. Although my father did not benefit from any formal education, through his initiative, members of his male and unmarried female lineage through generations to a very large extent are now able to easily identify themselves by name anywhere in the world. However, the children of our married female siblings naturally answer their fathers' last names. To this day, this has become a benchmark which most families follow.

While I was writing this book, I stumbled on a post by my Niece, Angela, in the family Group WhatsApp Social Medium. She gave a testimony (so to speak) of how the family name "Eigbobo" opened a door of opportunity for her while she was in her final year at Auchi Polytechnic.

"Permit me to give a brief testimony on how our family name (Eigbobo) saved me while I was at Auchi Poly". She wrote.

"I was not impressed with my final year result because my best course (Matrix) was tampered with and that affected my grade; so, I refused the result and decided to investigate what happened." She continued. "The officer in the Examiner's office initially refused to attend to me but when on his enquiry I told him my last name, he asked,

"do you know .... Eigbobo?"

"He is my uncle." I replied.

That calmed him down and he took pains to check the master list in his office. At last he discovered that there was an error. After It was corrected, my position that was seventh on the result sheet was adjusted to third! I took time to narrate this story because there is nothing like family name," she concluded.

The above scenario thus justified a projection made by my uneducated father in 1961 - more than **fifty years ago**, - when he advised us his children to effect a change of our last name!

THE ILLNESS AND TRANSITION OF MY FATHER

For as long as I could remember while I was growing up, my dad had battled arthritis and, what I was later to find out was, kidney problem. When I was about sixteen years old the ordeal of my having to take him on a bicycle a few times for traditional treatment at Oghagbo-Opoji, Ishan in Nigeria through a largely undulating topography is still fresh in my memory. Until then I had never seen an adult cry, but when I saw my dad shed tears from the pains of the numerous incisions and peppery concoction scrubbing on his knees and legs, I could not help also crying. It was a very sad moment for me. I happened to know that prior to and after that, he had also sought treatment in many hospitals including University College Hospital, Ibadan without a solution.

While I was working in Lagos, I brought him to Lagos in 1974 to receive treatment at Ajayi Memorial Hospital after which he returned home looking healthy. On learning that he was sick again one year later, I had planned to go home to bring him to Lagos again but because I too took ill and could not drive the over three hundred kilometers distance, I arranged for him to travel by airplane from Benin City. I picked him up from the airport in Lagos and took him again to Ajayi Memorial Hospital. He was examined and immediately hospitalized. After intensive treatment, he appeared to be recovering but suddenly exactly one week later, on Sunday September 7, 1975, my dad lost life's final battle and joined his ancestors at the age of eighty-two years. I remember asking the doctor after what in my opinion was a sudden end, even though he was on admission at the hospital.

"Doctor, what happened, why did he die? He looked okay last night."

"His kidneys suddenly stopped working and when that happens, there is nothing a doctor can do." He replied.

"He was a very good patient and the nurses liked him." He added.

Four days later, the remains of my father were taken to my hometown, Irrua in Bendel State (now Edo State) in Nigeria for interment.

ANNUAL EASTER FAMILY REUNION

After my father joined his ancestors, we the children under the leadership of our eldest brother, Sunday, decided to keep faith with his legacy, notwithstanding the huge expansion of his lineage thus far. Therefore, immediately the interment ceremony was concluded in November 1975, we all agreed not to allow the transition of our father to bring an end to the family unity he so much desired and tirelessly worked for during his lifetime.

Easter period being the only time we were all sure to observe four consecutive non-working days each year (Good Friday through Easter Monday), I suggested the idea of annual Easter family reunion at the family house which I envisioned would not only be to the benefit of us children, but also all the Eigbobo family descendants nationwide. The first of such gatherings at Easter of 1976, the first year after our late father transited, turned out to be a phenomenal success; it brought together not only my siblings but also my late father's grand and great-grandchildren from all over Nigeria. We even had the pleasure of hosting some of the spouses of our sisters who accompanied their wives to celebrate Easter with our family members.

It was a happy reunion which provided a platform for our children and grandchildren who lived very far apart within Nigeria to meet, some for the first time in their lives, and interact freely. At the end they exchanged contact addresses and opened lines of communication. To keep the momentum going in the minds of my siblings and isolate the possible thought of the financial implication for subsequent Easter gatherings, I offered to, and did in fact continue to bankroll all expenses for our gatherings, less transportation, for the next ten years. That helped a great deal to encourage all concerned to look forward to each subsequent gathering. The Easter reunion has continued to this day, forty-two years after. However, as the euphoria of the initial enthusiasm died down and the family lineage lengthened, coupled with the biting economic downturn, attendance is no longer total as in the past. Nevertheless, I take consolation in the fact that some other families in my village have since embraced the Eigbobo family initiative.

The impact of the family annual reunion among us the children was such that it was on the night of the traditional funeral ceremony of my late stepmother that some of the mutual friends of her son, John and I knew that we were not born by the same woman. That was because of the close affinity between us growing up, and the respect we had for our mothers, even though they were constantly in cold war for no tangible reasons other than that they were married to the same husband.

But my half-brother and I were always seen together; being kids that we were, we did have our own share of occasional squabbles, but we hardly ever fought or even quarreled openly growing up. John was less than one year older than me, but I respected him like he was a father to me because that was the way we were raised, and our father did not expect anything less. That was the family into which I was born and in which I grew up.

BENEFIT OF MY FATHER'S LEGACY

Many years after we completed elementary school education, John continued as a school teacher in Ishan Division and I worked in a bank in Lagos. Both of us were already married at the time and were raising our own families. Each time I was coming home, I would first drive to wherever he was teaching in Ishan to announce my arrival before driving to our village. I remember clearly that on one occasion several years after the transition of our father, I visited home while I was on annual vacation and observed that a goiter was growing on my half-brother's neck.

By the way, John was the only son of his mother amid four of us from my mother. Without waiting for him to talk to me about the strange growth, I asked him if he could come to Lagos to undergo a procedure to remove it before it assumed life threatening dimension. He complained of the possible cost and I assured him that he didn't have to bother himself about the cost. He agreed, and we planned to not let our mothers know exactly why he was coming, because we believed that neither of them seemed positioned to repose confidence in our ability to show genuine mutual love and concern for one another's welfare.

Just as we had planned it, John came to Lagos during one of his school holidays and had the procedure. The enormity of the procedure exceeded my expectation; it lasted four good hours! My wife and I were not allowed into the operating theater and after about two hours waiting time, I became very nervous and scared.

"Why is it taking so long, has something gone wrong?" I asked in soliloquy as Christiana and I anxiously paced back and forth at the corridor of the facility – becoming agitated. Almost four hours later, I was invited in to see my brother; my heart beat fast as I sat by his bedside. The anesthesia had not completely worn out. The doctor, who was our good family friend, told me to call his name.

"Brother John," I called him, "are you ok?"

"Yes," he said in a clear tone, and the doctor told me that the procedure was successful.

My brother did not speak further but when I held his hand, he looked up at my face and smiled. I was ecstatic and said, "thank you, Lord."

"Why did it take so long doctor?" I asked.

"The visible goiter which was growing outward on the left side of the neck was even smaller than an invisible one growing inward on the right, and so we decided to operate on both sides." She explained.

For obvious reasons, I waited for the scares of that surgery to heal completely before allowing my brother to return home. His mother was pleased to see him without the goiter but that did not restrain her from reminding her son that he took a risk by undertaking such a trip without her prior approval.

"Remember that you are my only male child in this house," she reminded him.

My mother, on the other hand, though happy at what I did for my half-brother, also took me to task on what she considered a risk that I took without first talking to her.

"Do you know that anything could have happened to your brother, during that operation and had he not survived it, his mother would have thought you deliberately planned to remove him from your midst?" she asked me.

"Do these women know that we are now adults?" I imagined and was nonchalant. I couldn't, however, help but flash my mind back to the protracted surgery as she spoke, and without giving away my emotions, I inwardly again thanked God that everything went well. My brother and I later discussed our mothers' comments and decided to ignore them. Such was the level of mutual suspicion among wives in some polygamous homes, ours not excluded.

SELFISH PERCEPTION ABOUT THE GIRL CHILD EDUCATION.

At the time of my birth, not many female children were given the opportunity to attend school in my part of the country due to the selfish belief then that the role of the girl child should only be to stay at home and support her mother until she was old enough to be married away into another family. Even in families that could afford the cost, it was thought not necessary to spend such resources to educate a girl.

Comfort, my elder sister is three years older than me and, if she was a boy, she might have been in school three years ahead of me. When I was enrolled in school, she could not understand why she too was not enrolled and she was sad. To pacify her, my father decided to instead enroll her in the domestic science center in the same school which I was to attend, to learn needlework and dressmaking. That meant that we could go to school together in the morning and return together after school hours. Such an arrangement was however considered in some families as a luxury which they could not afford.

In some other families, as it was with the girl child, even a first son was not allowed to attend school at that time because of the perception that he was expected to accompany his father to the farm. He had, as a first son, to be acquainted with and superintend over his father's farmlands and other economic crops which would be part of his inheritance after the death of his father. However, for him to qualify to inherit his father's family house (Ijogbe), he had to be financially able to lead the younger siblings to undertake the traditional final burial rites of their late father which normally entailed seven days performance of traditional rites.

If for any reason he died without fulfilling that obligation, the responsibility for the final burial rites fell on the next eldest male child alive in the family who would then be entitled to their father's inheritance. He too should be able to undertake their father's final burial rites before his own death, otherwise, the chain of responsibility could go on and on until one surviving eldest son performed the burial rites.

In my family, for instance, my father did not go to school either because his father could not afford the cost of his enrolment or because he was in any event a first son who must accompany him to the farm. My father though not educated was, however, relatively civilized having had the privilege to work as a court messenger. He told me that the unfolding events had helped him to make up his mind to introduce all his male children to formal education up to at least First School Leaving Certificate level. That would enable us to learn how to speak, read and write the English language and strengthen us economically. He achieved that; all my male siblings and I subsequently went through and completed our elementary school education.

Out of the five boys my father gave birth to, only one, my immediate younger brother, Michael benefited from a secondary school education after completing his elementary school education. He had that privilege because he is nine years younger than me and at the time he completed his elementary school education, my elder brother Sunday, and I were already in employments. We were thus financially strong enough to jointly fund Michael's secondary school education until he went on to obtain the West African School Certificate. He joined me in Lagos and took up appointment with the Federal Ministry of Finance. He was subsequently transferred to the Nigerian Customs Service where he retired as a Superintendent of Customs.

Unfortunately, among my female siblings, it was only my elder sister Comfort, who missed attending elementary school. All the other female children who were born after her had the opportunity to attend school because western civilization had started to spread in their time; therefore, more girls were enrolled in elementary schools. The introduction of free primary school education subsequently by the then Western Region government in Nigeria also resulted in reducing the level of mass illiteracy in the region. It helped to a large extent to change the perception in most families where the girl child might not have been allowed to attend school.

As I have already mentioned, my father worked as a court messenger which was what took him to Ubiaja, where I was born. He later left that job and secured another one as a Mail Runner with Posts & Telegraphs Department (now Nipost), under the Federal ministry of communications. He later earned promotion to the position of Office Messenger before he retired in 1964. I had no idea why and how he left his first job.

In retrospect, I am convinced that my dad might have been a very smart child at school had he benefitted from a formal education. When I was growing up, I used to watch in amazement his ability to communicate with his colonial expatriate bosses at work without the help of any interpreter, and without even the benefit of elementary school education! He could understand "king's" English but could only speak what was known as "pigin" English. Desirous to not thumb-print on his pay voucher monthly, my father also learnt on his own how to write and sign his name while receiving his monthly salary!

My mother even though not educated was, like most of her peers, very hard working. She engaged in the trade of, among other things, frying gari, a staple food which she processed from cassava and she walked several miles to various markets in the surrounding villages and towns to market the finished product.

Other means of transportation then were scarce and very expensive, if at all available. When my father retired and returned to his village my mother engaged in farm work, planting fruits and vegetables, e.g. cassava, pepper, tomatoes, okra and groundnuts wherever my father cultivated a farm annually, which she harvested for family consumption and marketing purposes.

THE ART OF SPINNING & WEAVING.

My mother was very good with the art of spinning raw cotton into strings of thread with which she weaved calico, a plain-woven textile material made from unbleached and often not fully processed cotton. In fact, I started school with the calico woven by my mother and sewn to a shirt and a pair of short pants.

COMMUNAL LIFE IN MY VILLAGE.

At the time I was born, my village Idumebo in Irrua, Ishan in Edo State of Nigeria consisted of not more than twenty-five families of mainly contiguous subsistent indigenous farmers who lived a communal life style where everybody was his brother's keeper. We were told that all the families were inter-related one way or another, their forefathers having migrated from Benin City, the state capital of the present Edo State, in Southern Nigeria.

For instance, I recall as a little boy in the early 1940s, a fight broke out between my village and the neighboring Ebhoakhuala village in Ekpoma Town, Ishan Division in Western Nigeria over the ownership of a piece of farming land to which cutlasses and other farming implements were deployed. An alarm was raised, and all able bodied young men and adults mobilized to the battle ground in defense of the village asset even though the land in question belonged to only a few of the families in my village. In the ensuing encounter, some of our villagers were injured, and they were all treated by the community at no cost to their families. Such was the level of unity and brotherhood that existed then in my village.

Good upbringing of children was not seen as belonging only to their biological parents. Therefore, any child stepping out of line was summarily disciplined by any adult present, provided, of course, that such action was taken in good faith without prejudice, in the best interest of the community and the wellbeing of the child. The child's parents did not question the adult's authority to discipline their child.

Construction of a mud house belonging to any member of the community from foundation to roofing level involved every able bodied young man, through communal effort, at no cost to the owner of the property. All that the owner was expected to do was to provide food for the workers at the end of each working day. It also created avenues for children from different families to interact and get to know each other. Children and young adults were taught to respect the elderly. If a boy or girl saw an elderly person carrying any load of whatever sort, as a mark of respect, he or she was obliged, without prompting, to take it over from the elder.

Long before I was born, my village had been a predominantly traditional community and was tacitly unaccommodating of the Christian religion; no church existed there for many years. That was because the indigenes worshipped a deity called "Unoko." There was a festival called "Ilunoko" which was celebrated big annually and was usually ushered in with a carnival. All the village indigenous maidens, irrespective of age, wearing only beads around their waists, and men young and old clad in warlike attires but in peaceful celebration danced from the village square to pay homage to the "Onogie," the traditional ruler of Irrua Town. The villagers saw 'Ilunoko' festival as equivalent to Christmas or any other Christian festival.

Modern civilization has, however, since helped to tone down the intensity of the deity worship particularly the carnival. The succeeding generations became more and more educated and they imbibed western civilization. What used to be a proud heritage of the villagers gradually became looked upon by the new generation of children born into the village as old fashioned or even primitive. The result is that New Generation churches of various denominations now spring up in their numbers in all the nukes and corners of the village. The village itself has also become enlarged in the number of indigenes through family reproduction over the years, and their accommodation of strangers. Christianity has taken a firm root among the inhabitants, both indigenes and strangers alike and at least more than ninety percent of the village residents could be said to identify with Christianity as I write this book.

Additionally, the citing of a Federal Specialist Teaching Hospital, and a Federal Grains Reserve Silo in the village by the Federal government, has resulted in the influx of strangers from different towns, states and even countries into the village. Many of them now live and work in and around the village, and many aspects of tradition hitherto peculiar to the villagers are fast giving way to modernity.

That congruity among the indigenous villagers has thus gradually become elastic as strangers buy land, build houses and live in them among the indigenes. It is only a matter of time before the village would become fully cosmopolitan in nature and many of the traditions hitherto seen as the exclusive preserve of the natives might completely fall away, or at least consigned to history.

The Journey So Far   AN AUTOBIOGRAPHY

CHAPTER 1

The family into which I was born was a nominal Christian one at the time of my birth, and because none of my parents went to church regularly at that time, they could not show us the way there while we were still kids. Attending a government school later where emphasis was not placed on religion or even going to church on Sundays, did not help matters for me and my siblings.

Our main contact then with God's word therefore was through the infrequent visits by expatriate female evangelists from Assemblies of God Mission church Eko-Ewu also in Ishan Division, Benin Province of Western Nigeria, who came to preach to us the word of God at Government School, Irrua. I was already close to my 'teen years then and, to those of us who did not have strong Christian backgrounds, we perceived it as just a subject in the school curriculum designed mainly to assist us to pass our religious knowledge examinations. While we were just irreligious kids who did not strongly believe in any religion, we knew that God created us even if we had yet no intimate relationship with Him. We were non-the-less taught at home to be honest, disciplined and respectful, especially to elders. That was considered very important for us.

"Stand up in the presence of the aged, show respect for the elderly and revere your God. I am the Lord." lev.19: 32

One good thing we had going for us was that we were not wayward even though we were not from a strong Christian background. Our parents knew about God and talked to us about Him but just did not know enough themselves to lead us, the children, to have intimate relationship with Him early in our formative years. That was mainly the reason why I did not give my life to Christ until very late in my life. Thanks to my wife Christiana (of blessed memory) whom God used later to lead me to salvation. Choosing eternal life ultimately has been, and will remain, the best decision of my life.

Like most of his peers, my father did not have the opportunity to attend school in his time, but he appreciated the value of education because of his exposure while he worked as a court messenger. His desire therefore, was to give each of his male children an early start at school. He had wanted me, for instance, to start elementary school early but was disappointed when I was refused admission at a young age just because my right-hand fingers could not touch my left ear, over my head.

That was the strict acid test in those years to determine the readiness of a child to be admitted into what was then known as infant class one, particularly in government schools. My father said his pleas that I was matured enough to start school were ignored because of the strict adherence to laid down rules at that time. Because my father did not want me to attend a missionary school - since many of those around terminated at elementary standard four - I had to wait another three years before I could gain admission at the age of nine years into the government school! Even at that age, I was still one of the youngest in my class.

On the home front, because my father enrolled all his boys in school as he had decided to do, he told me that he was mocked by some of his kinsmen.

"We shall see who will help him to maintain his farm; all his male children are in school", they would say

Ironically, when some of my siblings including myself completed elementary school education and started to work, the same kinsmen who had mocked my father became envious of him even before we became financially strong enough to commence sending any money to our father! That was brought about by a belated realization that at least educating male children, if you won't all children, was a good decision.

My father was the first son of his own father and to under-score his value for education, which he was denied, he did not hold back from us the history of how he tried to attend school but was withdrawn by his father because he was his first son and was expected to accompany him to the farm. In protest, my father found himself a job as a court messenger to avoid being only a full-time farmer.

POWER OF KNOWLEDGE/EDUCATION

Filled with indignation that he could not attend school, and because of his strong desire that somebody must be educated in the family, he told me that he withdrew one of his younger half-brothers from his father and enrolled him in school. He thus incurred the displeasure of his father who was unhappy with him, not only for refusing to follow him to the farm, but also for taking away his son from him, to attend school. He told us his father never forgave him for that singular action for the rest of his life.

Incidentally, his younger brother was very smart at school. When he completed his elementary school education, he proceeded to attend a one-year Extension Class nine miles away from home. On completion, he secured an appointment as a teacher and taught in many schools in Benin Province. By dint of hard work and determination, he went on, that time under his own initiative and expense, to attend a teachers' training college. Subsequently, through correspondence tuition, he also studied for and obtained a Bachelor of Science degree without the benefit of a formal secondary school or university education. He later worked as Vice Principal in a Government Teachers' Training College.

After obtaining his first degree and he had achieved much in the teaching profession, "uncle," (as I always call him) resigned from his employment in the school environment and went on to work in one of the Regional Ministries in Ibadan. He later quit the ministry job to pick up appointment with the Central Bank of Nigeria, Lagos, Nigeria in the early nineteen sixties. While at the Central Bank, he again obtained the Institute of Bankers' examination, (AIB part 11) qualification which, in addition to the bachelor's degree, accentuated his progress in Central Bank, culminating to his rise to the position of a Deputy Director before he retired.

"Uncle," now over ninety years old, today enjoys the distinction of being not only the first of the now numerous university & polytechnic graduates in my family but also one of the first two in my entire village. Unfortunately, his father did not live long enough to witness that laudable achievement to be able to forgive and possibly thank his son, my father, for his foresight in supporting his brother to go to school at the time he did.

It is not the intention here to only acquaint the reader with just what a determined self-effort could achieve in the life of a young person. Also, more important is how, conversely, the absence of necessary early enough knowledge and guidance, could limit a young person's potential achievements in setting and meeting goals.
For instance, even without attending a formal secondary school or university, my uncle went ahead to

earn a bachelor's degree because he received enough motivation from the teaching profession to set for himself long term goals towards which he worked. On the other hand, I, lacking the necessary early guidance, limited my own horizon because I overlooked the long-term benefit of basic academic qualification and focused only on the short-term goal of initial financial reward. I only concentrated on equating the achievements of my elementary school classmates instead of striving to achieve the best that I could be. I later found out that such amounted to shortsightedness. Although my goal was achieved, it was not sufficient to move me fast and very far enough as I progressed in service.

However, my short-term goal achieved its set objective since it helped me to initially move ahead of some of my peers who benefited from secondary or technical school education before they took up appointments in the Nigerian civil service. While their starting basic salary was one hundred & forty-six pounds per annum at their entry points, mine in the bank was two hundred pounds per annum, one year before they even left school. By the time they graduated from secondary school, my emolument was already more than two hundred and forty pounds per annum. In addition, I was able to secure employment in the biggest bank in the country because of my conscious effort not to be left behind. I short circuited them, so to speak, through studying shorthand and typewriting which for me became a necessity.

Laudable as that achievement sounded, that was as far as the comparison could go because some of them gradually progressed faster and overtook me subsequently because of their superior basic educational background. For instance, one of my elementary school peers who was fortunate to attend a technical school enlisted in one of the arms of the Nigerian armed forces as a cadet officer in training, armed with a Higher National Diploma. He traveled to the United Kingdom for his military training the same year I secured employment in Bank of West Africa Limited as a stenographer.

At the time he returned to Nigeria six years later, his commencing salary was below what I was already earning in the bank but, because of his superior basic educational qualification and training, he progressed faster and overtook me before long. He was also able to build a career in the Armed Forces and, in fact, rose to be Vice President of our country during his thirty-five years' service. But because of the lower basic educational qualification I possessed, the initial advantageous head start was soon eroded even though I was also able to advance to a senior management position in my thirty-four years service with the bank at the time I retired.

Comparatively, I made enviable progress in my own

employment, but that was only made possible by my consistent diligent on-the-job performance. Had I benefited from a motivation to back that up with higher academic qualifications while in the service of the bank, even without a secondary school or university education, I might have advanced faster and farther in my career before I retired. That was one short sighted decision I made from a lack of knowledge or counseling which hurt my rate of growth in service years later. That experience, however, helped me to shape the future of my own kids.

My father initially limited education to only his male children, and only through elementary school. My own modest educational qualification motivated me to resolve that all my male and female kids who were willing and able would be encouraged morally and financially to attain a minimum academic qualification of a first degree, or it's equivalent, before they ventured into other endeavors of their choice. To God be the glory, that helped to create a strong enough take off platform for those of them who were ambitious to build on to reach their God ordained potentials.

While I am on this journey, I continue to learn that the first motivation for achieving great things in life is knowledge. What follows is the will to translate that knowledge into unrelenting tenacity to succeed against all odds. Nothing good comes easy and raising the living and educational standard of a family requires the joint effort, sacrifice and commitment of both the parents and their children.

Part of my twenty-five years "long service award" in First Bank was a flight ticket to the United Kingdom for a two weeks vacation; it could, however, be commuted to cash, in need. That was to be my first air trip outside my country and I had looked forward to savoring that benefit. However, when the time to enjoy it came, considering that many of my kids were already in secondary schools, I decided that the money could be more beneficial if channeled towards their education than for me to engage in the pleasure of flying to the United Kingdom. I put that opportunity on hold and commuted to cash the cost of the return flight ticket. The consideration was that if my children were well educated and had good jobs, chances were that they might later be able to sponsor my travels to any country of my choice in the whole world, if I expressed a desire to travel.

To God be the glory, as I write these memoirs, I am doing so in the United States of America, where I currently live with one of my daughters, Obehiaye who lives and works here with her spouse. She and her sibling, Isedua, have done very well to build on the first-degree education each of them had acquired and they are conveniently coping with my upkeep and healthcare needs. I believe they and their other siblings are ever willing to receive and care for me now that I am aging, presumably because of reciprocal impetus to my own self-denial for the sake of uplifting the family overall standard while they were growing up.

In our clime, no matter the age of kids, they lived under their parents' roofs with full parental care for as long as it took them to either get married or find their bearing after their first-degree education. Most parents in Africa still enjoy the luxury to live with their kids in their old age, while the kids are very happy to have them around, if the need arises, instead of letting the parents move into assisted or old peoples' homes and abandoned there when they most need their children's companionship, care and attention.

That could be the difference between the African family heritage and, to a large extent, that of the western world where the law recognizes a child on attaining a certain age as an adult when he/she must either move out of the parents' home and/or fend for himself/herself even if he/she was permitted to live with them. Legally, the child could refuse to be subjected to parental control. It is not uncommon to hear children remind their parents,

"I am over eighteen dad/mum."

Also, not many of such kids are keen to integrate into their nuclear families the welfare of their parents at their old age. Perhaps, that's the reason why you have more western world seniors than their African counterparts living in old people's homes, where the affinity to family members does not exist, except through infrequent visits by those of their family members who care to see them.

CHAPTER 2

EARLY EDUCATION/PARENTAL CONTROL

I had my elementary school education at Government School, Eguare-Irrua, and later, at St James's Anglican Primary School, Eguare-Opoji, both in Ishan Division of Benin Province now (Esan Central Local Government Council Area) of Edo State, Nigeria and obtained my First School Leaving Certificate in December 1953.

While I was growing up, I had developed interest in football (now called soccer.) Football was in its infancy then, at least in our clime, and was mostly a schools' sport played largely by boys for physical fitness and sometimes on competitive basis. The highest rewards when played on organized competitive basis were usually a small trophy called gold cup for the winning team, and silver cup for the runner up. Unlike now, footballs were made from semi processed leather and needed a lot of energy to kick around because of the weight once they had soaked water when played on wet surfaces. And football was played then without cleats.

My father had already secured his second job as Mail Runner and his salary was five shillings per month from which he regularly paid school fees totaling one shilling and six pence for his sibling, my uncle, (six pence) and three of his own biological sons, Sunday (six pence), John and Gilbert (myself), (three pence each) every term. Because we were all attending school, it became imperative that our dad had to cultivate a farm annually to supplement his salary to be able to adequately take care of his wives, including his father's widow, which became his responsibility after his father joined his ancestors, and his own numerous biological children. But how did we maintain the farm since he worked, and all his sons were in school?

My father adopted a strategy which worked well for the family. He arranged for all his sons to go and work in his farm after school hours each week-day, and we worked full days on week-ends. Often there was no lunch for us at home upon return from school; rather we would take off our school uniforms and proceed to the farm where our lunch would be ready, most times roasted yam with red palm oil. We all had our portions of work marked out for each day. That was the only way to ensure that we produced enough food for the family throughout the year.

That arrangement disappointed those of my father's kinsmen who had expected him to come and buy farm produce from them, particularly yams, during harvest simply because all his sons were in school and he was also working. They often waited in vain and could not understand how we were surviving. Because of my father's planning ability, we were always self-sufficient in food production and even sometimes harvested enough produce to have excess to take to the local markets to sell.

However, helpful as such an arrangement was, it did not leave me with any room to advance my interest in football because I had no time to attend practice. I recall that the only once I complained about not being allowed time to attend football practice, my father retorted and asked me, "have you ever heard of anybody who went to England through playing football?" Of course, he was right, because I had not known any at that time. In any event, football then in that part of Nigeria was only played for pleasure and prestige, even when competitive. It was not a paying profession as it is today - a lucrative business for professional soccer, not only for players and organizers, but also for nations. What a transformation! How I wish my father is alive today to see professional soccer players flying around the world in their private jets, investing in multi-million-dollar businesses, enjoying comfortable living standards through soccer and garnering fame.

MISSED OPPORTUNITIES

It was my intention to sit for an entrance examination after my elementary school education in 1953 to enable me to proceed to a secondary School in Benin City. The entrance fee was two shillings and six pence, and my father had earlier reluctantly agreed to give me the money for registration. He later became encouraged to withhold it because my mother had ignorantly said, "I think it will be too much for him to go to school for another five years without working to earn any money."

It was obvious that she spoke from the heart and, viewed from her stand point, she believed that what she said was the best for her son's future.

That was all the support my father needed to change his mind - and he did. I merely exhibited attitude since it was not politic then to argue with our parents. To placate me, I remember that my father gave to me one six penny coin out of the money. (a six-penny coin amounted to a lot of money for a child of my age then, an equivalent of school fees paid by an upper class elementary school pupil for one whole term!)

For instance, out of the three tenths (called 'anini') my mother often gave me to eat lunch at school each day, I only bought food for two tenths (anini) which was often enough for me to eat and share with friends who did not have money to buy food. 'One penny' was made up of ten tenths (anini); so, the six pence my father gave to me amounted to sixty tenths!

My father later offered me in addition a choice between taking up a teaching appointment in an elementary school at home (like my immediate elder half-brother, John did after completing his elementary school education), and proceeding to Lagos to join my eldest brother, Sunday. He himself had enlisted in the Nigeria Police Force after obtaining his First School Leaving Certificate in 1950. I opted to go to Lagos in the vain hope that I might be able to convince my brother to let me proceed further in my education.

In those days, unless you grew up in a city like Lagos or any of the other big cities in Nigeria, the perception was that the only easily available employments to First School Leaving Certificate holders were either to enlist in the Nigeria Police Force or teach in a local elementary school. Neither of these two appealed to me and I was then released to go to Lagos.

I arrived in Lagos, Nigeria on January 11, 1954 and was pleased to be able to persuade my brother to let me go into Trade Center, Yaba, Lagos. Admission into my favored institution, Technical Institute, Yaba, had already closed. He agreed; then the unexpected happened. I attended the selection interview which usually preceded the writing of the entrance examination. While I was on the queue, some of us were told to step out of the line because we were considered too tall. No one listened to any explanation neither did anyone bother to know how old we were. It was all about our heights. I was only eighteen years old then but was very tall for my age.

I had delayed in gaining admission into elementary school several years back for being "too young" and then again failed to gain admission into Trade Center that time for being 'too tall.'

"This is frustrating." I said to myself.

That was my last hope to advance beyond elementary school and, predictably, my elder brother said to me, "now we have to go in search of employment!"

My opportunity to attain higher education thus came to an end.

Had I been raised in the city, I might have known that there were other avenues open to me and that I could still have advanced farther in education without necessarily attending a university or even a secondary school. But the awareness was non-existent in the village, and opportunities were few at that time.

In retrospect, I have discovered that life is full of learning curves. Sometimes, there are things you get to have an opportunity to change but there are others you just look back on with nostalgia, mostly in your twilight years, and wish you had done them differently; but you discover that you cannot turn back the hands of the clock.

I am over eighty-one years old now and I harbor no regret because to the best of my ability, I utilized my strengths and skills to take advantage of the possible opportunities available to me compatible with my environment. I believe that I achieved a measure of success along the path through which I had traveled considering all the limitations and obstacles along the way.

We must all have made mistakes in our lives and the lessons we have learned from our failures and successes can help those coming behind. There are much the young can learn from those who have traveled the distance to enable them to avoid the inevitable pitfalls along the way.

The young people nowadays should count themselves lucky that they have access to all the technological advancements, which make life easier for them, an impetus which we lacked. All the things that we undertook as children and young adults manually in our time are now either mechanically or electronically performed, and with the likelihood that more scientific inventions are continually tested out. The rate at which technology is moving, a day would come when the human brain would become totally dormant and invented machines would take over all it's functions.

I see my two little grandkids who just entered Middle School in the United States come home with laptops issued to them at school; thanks to advancement in technology. In my time in Nigeria, even while I was already working in the bank, there were only two manually operated old cash register adding machines in the branch of the bank where I worked. A good number of the staff would queue up for their use. They were both in the custody of the Chief Clerks in the branch who decided who could use the machines at any given time. It did not matter to them if a ledger keeper had ten pages of hand-written ledger entries or more to cast each day.

If the answer to your request for the use of any of the adding machines was a 'no', you had to go and manually cast your entries until you balanced your ledger for that day. His refusal to let you use the machine would not be accepted as an excuse for your ledger not being balanced! If it took you all day and night to balance your ledger, so be it and no overtime pay was available. If that happened, you would just go to the water tap the following morning, wash your face, and resume work for the new day without the opportunity to go home and freshen up. You had to be available to attend to the bank's customers as from eight o'clock in the morning! That was the unwritten rule in the bank in my generation.

CHAPTER 3

SEARCH FOR EMPLOYMENT

I had learned to make my own decisions at a very early age and realizing that I was not born with a silver spoon in my mouth, and I could not proceed beyond elementary school educationally, I prepared myself to take up any job with the sole aim of earning money. I had started by seeking casual jobs at building construction sites in Lagos where I engaged in all sorts of tough menial jobs that were stressful for a child of my age, just to earn some money while my peers were in school. So tough was the building construction site work that I often had nightmares in my sleep about the work I did during the day, and that made me feel sad and irritable. But I knew I had to work to be able to earn money of my own to meet some necessary commitments.

After I lost the opportunity to go further in education, I became so indignant that I momentarily lost focus because I had no plan 'B' then in my mind for the future. I was disoriented and became agitated. You would have thought then that the tedious jobs I did at the construction sites would compel me to fall for just any other employment. No, not me; the ordeal notwithstanding, I had the temerity to turn down my brother's entreaty to enlist in the Nigeria Police Force. I did not know then that even at a time I had struggled with having intimate relationship with God, He was guiding me in all my thoughts and the decisions I made. I was not yet a true Christian, but I knew that The Lord was walking with me.

I had lived with my brother at Obalende barracks for many months and had observed a few things about the life of a typical Nigeria policeman. His pace of advancement was slow; for instance, when I arrived in Lagos in 1954, my elder brother, Sunday, had already served over three years after leaving the police Training College, and he was still a constable! He had not earned a promotion. That, and because of the seemingly subservient behavior and stereotype nature of work that I observed was inherent in the Police Force, I was not enthused to be one, especially as I had made up my mind not to be left behind by my peers already in secondary schools. I saw myself as a young man in a hurry and felt that enlisting in the police force could be a drawback to me in realizing my ambition to get on the fast lane, my low educational attainment notwithstanding. I thus incurred the displeasure of my brother, Sunday, and he angrily said to me,

"if you are not ready to enlist in the Nigeria Police Force, you should prepare to return to the village."

For the first time in my life, I rebelled.

"I am prepared to leave your house brother but returning to the village is not an option." I replied.

Young and submissive as I was then, I had nevertheless developed thick skin when it came to making decisions affecting my future because I already had a mind of my own, and I believed that I knew what I wanted. My brother took a stern look at me and without saying one more word, he walked away. I could see a very surprised look on his face, perhaps, because I had never talked back at him before. Neither of us talked about that matter ever again. Many years later my brother and I got talking and he humorously told me that the way he heard me speak that day, he feared I could run away from the house and if I did, he could be in serious trouble with our parents, which was why he said he calmed down. I apologized to him and I also told him the reasons for my reaction back then. We both laughed over the conversation since we had individually moved on and I was already doing well in my employment with the Bank.

At the time, my brother did not know what was going through my mind. I did not tell him, for instance, that I was pre-occupied with the idea of what I could do that I would not be placed at a disadvantage, in terms of earning capacity. Five years down the road my peers who had the opportunity to proceed to secondary schools would have graduated and come out to work. Not earning less than them was the only barometer I used to measure how well I was doing. He did not know, for instance, that while he was taking job security into consideration in his advice to me to enlist in the police force, I was ignorantly consumed in the efficacy of "quick fixes." They did help initially for me to move ahead but the overall outcome turned out not to be enduring enough on the long run.

DECISION TO STUDY PITMAN'S SHORTHAND.

At the time I had the above altercation with my brother, I had already made up my mind to settle for studying shorthand and typewriting. I was convinced that I could read the books on my own within four years without going through any formal institution of learning. It would also not require much financial commitment. All that I believed I would need was my time and the ability to read and understand, and I would be there. At least, so I conceived in my small mind.

Earlier, I had the opportunity to stumble on a Pitman's shorthand Instructor and its Key in the possession of another "barrack boy" (as we were generally referred to). I convinced myself that I had seen in the two books what it would take to achieve my set objective. I had discreetly found out that shorthand typists were in high demand, but in short supply then both in the private and public sectors. The remuneration I also discovered was good, but because of the difficulty associated with studying shorthand perhaps because of its unorthodox outlines, not many young men wanted to venture into it. I had no qualms in my mind that if I worked hard and diligently, securing a good job as a stenographer would not be a problem.

I was excited but when I finally summoned the courage to inform my brother about the projection, he watered it down, refused to support it and therefore also refused to provide the money needed for the books. I saw all of that as a move to dampen my enthusiasm or even kill my interest in it; but nothing else appealed to me. I had made up my mind and not even my brother's refusal to help start me up could dissuade me. On the other hand, I could not blame my brother for his actions because I later found out that he did not know anything about Pitman's shorthand at the time.

Indignant, and without any money to buy the two books, I decided to intensify my efforts at seeking an apprenticeship position which I had earlier applied for with the engineering branch of Elder Dempster Lines Limited, a British shipping company located at Wilmot Point, Bar Beach, Lagos, in Nigeria as an apprentice fitter in their ships. I reported there walking back and forth from Obalende Police Barracks every working day for one month in the hope that my name would be listed for recruitment. When it became clear to me that they were not interested in recruiting, I stopped trying and made up my mind that I was ready to take up any employment primarily to raise money for my shorthand books.

CHAPTER 4

SECURING MY FIRST EMPLOYMENT

Having made up my mind to seek employment anywhere except, of course, the Nigeria Police Force, I applied to Messrs J.N. Zarpas & Co, a bus transport company in Lagos Metropolis. I was offered a job as "bus washer" on a daily wage of four Shillings – or six shillings, if I worked at night, but payable monthly. I accepted the offer and commenced work sometime in 1955.

"Why did I accept to do that work after I refused to enlist in the more dignifying job of a police officer?" you might ask.

I had planned it to be a stop-gap to where I envisaged I would be in four years, which was becoming a stenographer.

Bus washing, which by the way was totally manual, was a job meant largely for young men who did not go to school, and they were many in my time, but I accepted to take that job because of my strong desire to find the money to buy my shorthand books. The tedious work entailed each person washing the outside and cleaning the inside of six fifty-two-seater buses between nine o'clock pm. and four o'clock am. when on night shift, and a similar number during the day if available. We were also frequently issued with diesel to wash the engines of each bus, which later resulted in our developing rashes on the fingers, making it difficult for me to eat any food without cutleries. Yet, I refused to quit the job.

My salary per month was anything between six and seven pounds and it turned out that my first month's salary was more than enough to offset the cost of my dream shorthand books. I bought them and started to study at home when not at work and during recess at work. It was not easy learning shorthand on my own at home but because of the target I had set for myself, I found joy in perseverance and knew that once I could read and understand what I read, I could be successful.
Ironically, that employment lasted for only four months. Each of the three of us performing the duties received a letter from the personnel manager which read in part,
"in view of the current reorganization in the company, your services are no longer required," we were informed. No prior query was issued for any wrong doing, no warning, and we were gone. My colleagues who did not attend even elementary school were very upset at the outcome, but it only gave me food for thought and I asked myself. "Is this how I shall continue in Lagos?"
My zeal was reinforced, and my answer was "no".
Having that employment had served its purpose; that of acquiring my shorthand books. For me, therefore, losing the job was a blessing in disguise, and the motivation I needed to take my shorthand studies very seriously.
As at that time, my elder brother, Sunday, with whom I lived had been posted at short notice to Sapele in

Western Nigeria, (now Delta State) and I decided not to accompany him because I believed that there would be more opportunities available to me in Lagos than Sapele. A good friend of my brother, another policeman residing at Obalende police barracks was from the same village with us. He kindly offered to accommodate me. As things turned out, my living with him almost put him in trouble with the police authorities because it contravened an unwritten rule that forbade any police constable to harbor grown up boys in the police barracks. Many constables and non-commissioned officers did harbor their siblings, notwithstanding, but my host was unlucky to have been reported to the authorities by his apartment mate, presumably out of jealousy.

I happened to know about the rule because while I lived with my brother, barrack inspection was conducted on every first Saturday of the month. Every household would wake up as early as three or four o'clock in the morning to wash and clean up their living rooms, bedrooms, bathrooms, restrooms, kitchens and their surroundings. Thereafter, all the grown-up boys living in the barracks must quickly vacate the barracks before the inspecting police officer arrived by six o'clock in the morning. After the inspection, they were free to return to the barracks again until the next inspection date.

TRAUMATIC LIFE EXPERIENCE IN LAGOS.

Without a job, and in possession of only a small sum of money, I decided to move out of the barracks, against the entreaties of my brother's friend to stay, to save him any further embarrassment. I moved in with one of my cousins, Jacob, at Ijeh village near Obalende in Lagos Island of Nigeria under very harsh conditions. At Ijeh village, Jacob lived in a single room with one spinster as a co-tenant in a house structure built with bamboo stems and thatched roof. The lady, (whose name I cannot remember now), was covertly opposed to my living with them, even though all I did was come to sleep there at night. But she was hamstrung and could not stop me from living in the house because my cousin was the principal tenant.

Nevertheless, the lady remained tacitly hostile and made subtle attempts to force me out by washing dishes with pepper on them on the cemented floor where I slept on a mat every night. The outcome was that I developed body rashes arising from bites from bugs and worms because I repeatedly slept on the wet floor. I refused to be deterred and did not even complain to my cousin because, firstly, there was no immediate hope of alternative accommodation and, secondly, I was convinced that it would not be too long before I could rent my own room if I concentrated on my studies and was able to secure a stable employment.

I persevered and continued to live under the traumatic

conditions in the hope that she would someday relent. She never did, and I had to move out eventually. The cruel treatment meted out to me strengthened my desire to concentrate on the study of my books, and while all the ugly events were unfolding, I stuck with reading my shorthand books even more diligently.

RISE ABOVE MENIAL JOBS.

My unemployment status did not last for more than a few months before I secured another employment with a sole proprietorship undershirt manufacturing concern at Idoluwo Street, Idumagbo, Lagos. The salary was two pounds per month working ten hours shift daily including Saturdays and public holidays. My employer also operated another company for the export of ginger and pepper overseas and because he discovered that I was one of his only three educated employees, occasionally, he would move me to Apapa Port to work as a tally clerk for the export business without any extra remuneration.

While I worked there, I moved in with my uncle Lawrence who worked at the General Post Office, Marina, Lagos, to obviate the traumatic living conditions at Ijeh Village. My new employment again only lasted for a few months because one day, my employer just walked into the factory and said "the factory did not make any profit this month. Everyone of you should decide whether to be paid his full salary and quit or to accept half salary and continue to work here."

"What impudence, half pay from two pounds a month salary after such a tedious job? I sighed.

I could not see a future in that kind of employment because it sure sounded to me like slave labor. Along with a few other staff, I opted for my full salary and to quit. My employer was unhappy with those of us who so decided and ordered us to "go and collect your salaries and leave my factory immediately".

I was again back in the labor market.

Incidentally, I never felt bad each time I lost a job because it afforded me the impetus to devote more time to learning my shorthand and typewriting which I then saw as my only hope of outgrowing menial and casual jobs in the future in Lagos. I had saved some money to which I resorted for my upkeep while my unemployment lasted.

Because I devoted nearly all my available time to my studies, I observed that arising from my inability to engage in certain frivolities like going out to places like cinema theaters to watch movies any more, some of my friends were unable to see any benefit for them in my decision to study shorthand. They, like me were unable to go further in their education after their elementary school came to Lagos but without any plan for their future. After trying unsuccessfully to distract me, they abandoned me. I did not bother because I had a focus.

That was when I learned that you do not follow any friend who is not going anywhere, because when your life takes a wrong turn, you should remember that you're the one on the driving seat. I let them go because I had already set a timeline of five years to catch up with my elementary school classmates who would be completing secondary school about then. At that time too, I had enrolled for a part time course in secretarial studies, including typewriting at Royal Commercial Institute, Pike Street, Lagos. In any event, I was left with little or no time for unbeneficial outdoor activities.

Soon, I secured another job with Leventis Stores Fancy Shop at Marina, Lagos, in 1956 as a messenger on a salary of four pounds per month. I was only a few months old in that employment when an opening occurred within the store for the employment of a Sales Clerk. At my request, the Greek floor manager kindly allowed me to vie for the position with three other applicants from outside the store and, after a competitive test, I was selected to fill the vacant position and elevated to the position of a sales clerk. My salary was also increased to seven pounds ten shillings per month from four pounds. Not even that elevation could dampen my enthusiasm to continue to study stenography. I held on to that more dignified position until the middle of 1958, at which time I convinced myself that I had learned enough to be able to hold my own as a stenographer.

I then applied for employment simultaneously to Bank of West Africa Limited (Now First Bank of Nigeria Plc.), British & French Bank Limited (Now United Bank for Africa Plc.) and United Africa Company Limited (UAC). I was promptly invited for test and interview by both banks after which they both offered me employment having passed their competitive tests. To this day I cannot explain why I accepted to work for Bank of West Africa Limited, even when British & French Bank Limited salary at two hundred and ten pounds per annum was significantly higher than that of Bank of West Africa Limited at two hundred pounds per annum! I was also invited for a test by United Africa Company but because the date of their test coincided with the date I resumed work at Bank of West Africa Limited, I could not honor their invitation. The sacrifice I was making was beginning to yield results and with two job offers already and a tentative third, I was excited.

Two interesting scenarios also transpired. Out of the nine of us who started learning shorthand and typewriting at the same time, only three of us could reach a proficiency level to hold down a job. Similarly, out of the nine applicants invited for a test by Bank of West Africa Limited, I was to learn later that even though I was the only rookie, (the other eight were already experienced stenographers and each one of them was already working somewhere else), yet, I was the only one employed. It was the Grace of God at work in my life even when I was yet not serving Him properly.

Coincidentally, I accepted to work for Bank of West Africa Limited, I found out later that one of the other two was employed by British & French Bank Limited. The third had earlier secured employment with United Africa Company (UAC) T & T department, Iddo, all in Lagos. Remarkably too, all three of us later converted from Secretarial duties to clerical duties and rose to senior management positions in our respective employments.

CHAPTER 5

BREAKING NEW GROUND

After relinquishing a job by voluntary resignation from Leventis Stores as a sales clerk, I resumed work at Bank of West Africa Limited on July 13, 1958 as a stenographer for the first time. That change of job translated to a pay check leap from ninety pounds per annum, as a sales clerk at Leventis Stores, to two hundred pounds per annum as a stenographer at the bank, an increase of more than one hundred percent, in addition to my exuding the excitement of entering my dream profession. I was thrilled that I had moved ahead of my seemingly more fortunate elementary school classmates who were then still in their final year in secondary schools.

At the Bank at that time, the minimum basic educational qualification for employment as a full clerical Staff was a West African School Certificate or its equivalent General Certificate of Education, neither of which I possessed. However, stenography was regarded by the bank as specialized in nature because it was uncommon to find any West African School Certificate graduate then studying shorthand and typewriting. A First School Leaving Certificate as basic educational qualification, therefore, sufficed to employ stenographers and the job was remunerated in the bank on the same level with West African School Certificate.

That was how, through choosing the short-cut to study stenography, my commencing salary equated that of my peers who were not only one year ahead of me in elementary schools but had to graduate from secondary schools before being employed in the bank. I felt satisfied and fulfilled that not only had I met my target to not be left behind, even without acquiring a secondary school certificate, but I had, in fact, moved ahead of them.

With the new appointment came envy from those of my friends who had abandoned me when I struggled to make myself employable by shunning outings to the movie theatres. Rather than be happy for me, the fact that they knew my new pay check figure and where I worked elicited envy. At that time, some of them were still working as gatemen in business offices and private homes, and they had abandoned the study of stenography, which we started together, for being too difficult. I had always believed that there was a reward for hard work and I was determined to move away from friends whose association did not add value to me. I learned also that those who say it cannot be done shouldn't interrupt the people doing it.

REAPING THE FRUITS OF DILIGENCE

Part of the conditions of service attached to my new employment in the bank was a long probationary period of twelve months within which time, if my work and/or conduct were unsatisfactory, my appointment could be terminated without any notice. The branch where I worked was, and still is, the bank's main branch in Nigeria with a total staff strength then of over two hundred and fifty. Easily the highest in any branch of the bank, competition for advancement was inevitably intense.

While still serving my probation, however, my on-the-job performance had attracted the attention of the branch Accountant. A Briton, he had preferred that I, instead of the most senior stenographer (as I learnt was the normal procedure,) should be the one to provide relief for his secretary to enable him to proceed on his annual leave. His secretary was the senior Secretary in the Accounts Department while I was a junior probationer in the typing pool; I could not understand why I was selected ahead of at least six of my older confirmed colleagues. In any event, none of them envied me the assignment because the Accountant was perceived to be very fastidious, and almost every member of the secretarial staff tried hard to avoid working directly with him if it was possible. One needed to have one's wits about one to survive working with him, everyone seemed to believe!

Confident as I was that I could work with him, I could not help but feel a little nervous initially because I feared that if I failed to perform while working directly with a man on whose overall recommendation depended my suitability for confirmation, I could easily lose my job, being yet a probationer. Prior to confirmation, probationers in the Bank then were often jokingly taunted with "your name is still written in pencil and can be erased easily!"

I was not given any choice to accept or decline anyway, so I braced up for the assignment. At the end, I successfully completed the six weeks relief period unscathed and without blemish, but to be honest, those six weeks of my service were like forever because I was on edge throughout because of the responsibilities and the fear of stumbling. Happily, on my due date, my appointment was confirmed.

Just when I heaved a sigh of relief that I was successful in that assignment, and a few months after the confirmation of my appointment the Accountant recommended that I should also relieve the Assistant Manager's secretary who was due to proceed on leave. Here, the experience I gained while working with the Accountant became invaluable and gave me added confidence. The Assistant Manager's Secretary was a very senior stenographer but for reasons I could not understand then, he had accumulated four weeks' arrears of work at the time he commenced his leave. He also made a poor job of handing over to me. Although I did not complain, the Assistant Manager was aware of the arrears of work. As I battled to bring them up to date, he placated me with,

"Gilbert, don't worry, just do your best."

That, of course, spurred me to work harder, and at the

end, it paid off when the effort I put in later resulted to early appointment and subsequent promotion.

Within two weeks of my relief assignment, I had cleared the arrears and brought the work up todate. I was later to find out that the Secretary deliberately left the arrears to make me appear incompetent before his boss, a ploy to guarantee his return to the seat after his leave. Unfortunately, things did not work out as he had planned because, so impressed I believe the Assistant Manager was with my performance that he decided to re-assign his secretary while he was still on leave. His fears were confirmed, but the antics did not work.

"Gilbert," the Assistant Manager said, "I'll be pleased to replace my Secretary with you."

I did not respond since he was not asking a question, but I was discreetly indignant because I knew that I would not be paid the equivalent of the man's salary (which was more than twice my own) neither would any allowance be considered for my relieving well above my grade. There was no junior staff union or senior staff association in the bank at that time and no negotiated conditions of service existed. All conditions of service were unquestionably at the exclusive discretion of the Bank Management.

Besides, the Assistant Manager was another strict expatriate officer most members of the staff, both line bankers and stenographers, feared to cross his path. Indeed, just as he had told me, he instructed that his

Secretary should be reassigned upon his return from leave! I again successfully completed the relief assignment and was retained as the Assistant Manager's Secretary in 1961, ahead of all my seniors in the branch. A few years later, my position was designated Deputy Manager's Secretary consequent upon the new designation for the seat occupied by the Assistant Manager.

The Deputy Manager was a standing relief for the Manager during annual leave, and a scenario like the one that had resulted to my elevation played out again. The manager was to proceed on his annual leave and the Deputy Manager, was to relieve him. To ensure that he did not have to work with any other secretary, my boss arranged for the Manager's Secretary to also proceed on his leave. That arrangement thus created room for me to move along with him as relief for the manager's secretary, while his own relief assignment lasted. That phenomenon was repeated every single year for as long as he relieved the Manager until he was appointed District Manager, East and he had to move away from Marina Branch, Lagos, Nigeria.

FIRST PROMOTION & CONVERSION.

Exceeding my expectation of a double increment during the annual staff assessment in 1970, the new deputy Manager strongly recommended that I should be promoted to the Chief Clerk grade (now Supervisor). He

indicated in his recommendation inter alia,
"During the year, he exhibited the ability to perform more advanced work of following up routine correspondence from our diary system and to prepare follow-up letters, largely under his own initiative. He was also able to interview some of our small borrowing customers during the year whose knowledge of English is limited."

I was not very optimistic about the outcome of that recommendation at the time it was made but, Head Office accepted it and I was promoted to Chief Clerk grade (now Supervisor) effective January 1, 1971. I did not see that coming and it was remarkable because it became the first time that a secretarial staff would be promoted to the Chief Clerk grade while still working as a secretary typist in the branch.

The Secretary to the Manager Marina Branch was on his annual leave preparatory to retirement within a few months. While I was relieving him in 1971 the Manager, informed me that he would need me to replace his secretary. The branch management then recommended me for promotion to Officer Grade six (OG6), as a result, one year after my first historic promotion to Chief Clerk Grade. Perhaps, Head Office considering that it was too early for another promotion, instead awarded me a double increment and decided that I should first be moved from secretarial duties and deployed to the Head Office administration to supervise

Common Services Department.

That implied a conversion from secretarial duties to supervisory clerical duties; another privilege which no secretarial staff had enjoyed before then. My instinct told me that the Manager was not happy at the decision of Head Office to deprive him of my services as secretary, because he later said to me, "Gilbert, I was making my arrangements for you within this Branch, but Head Office have decided otherwise. I don't want them to post you to a dead-end job. If you do not find the Common Services supervisory duties challenging, do not hesitate to let me know."

But, of course, at the back of my mind, because I was happy to have been transferred from Secretarial duties to Clerical duties without me having to apply, I was determined to stick with that new assignment for whatever it was worth. I had earlier made up my mind not to ever request for any posting or refuse one.

DEPARTMENTAL MERGER

In a dramatic re-alignment of responsibilities within the Head Office, Common Services department, which I supervised, was merged with Printing & Stationery Department, Apapa, Lagos, and I had to move along with all the staff of Common Services department as Supervisor. Printing & Stationery department was established mainly to centralize the printing and supply of the bank's forms to all branches in Nigeria to minimize cost through bulk purchases of printing materials, and to maintain uniformity of forms utilized at all the branches of the bank throughout the country. The Manager of Printing & Stationery Department a Briton was due for his 1973 annual leave after Common Services Department which I supervised was merged with his department. In furtherance of the then on-going indigenization policy of the bank, he was also to proceed on a territorial transfer to Kenya in East Africa at the expiration of his leave in the United Kingdom. It became imperative that a Nigerian Printing & Stationery manager would be needed.

EXCEEDED EXPECTATION OF PROMOTION TO MANAGER

Knowing that the department did not function like a conventional banking branch, the manager recommended to Head Office, Lagos, the need to split it into two separate departments of Printing Department and Stationery & Supplies department, for checks and balances, each to be headed by a manager. He also recommended that because of the peculiar nature of the functions of the department, it would be preferable that personnel already working within should be appointed to head the two new departments. The transition, he said, would be easier because they were already conversant with the intricacies of its peculiar functions. Thus, he recommended the Assistant

Manager, who was already an officer and a professional printer, for appointment as Manager, Printing Department. He also recommended me, then the Senior Supervisor in Stationery & Printing department, for promotion to Officer grade six (OG 6), and to be appointed at the same time, Manager, Stationery & Supplies Department. One Assistant Manager was also recommended for each of the two new departments.

Expectedly, Head Office, Lagos advised that I should first be nominated to attend Officers' Course, but my boss told me that he stood his ground and succeeded in pushing his case with a strong recommendation that

"...he should be promoted without course because he is already carrying out the duties for which he is being recommended."

Head office then accepted the recommendations for the split and approved all the appointments. That approval again provided me with the unique privilege of being promoted to officer grade six (OG6) without course, and appointed manager on the same day - another "first" in the history of the bank. On confirmation as manager I was elevated to Officer Grade five (OG5) six months later.

Three years down the road in 1976, I requested for upgrading of Stationery & Supplies department Manager's position from Officer Grade five (OG 5) to (OG 4), since my opposite number in Printing Department was then already Officer Grade four (OG

4). The General Manager (Finance & Administration) later informed me that the Executive Director (Staff) turned down his recommendation because the ongoing upgrading process in the bank at the time was only for managers in conventional branch banking operations and not yet for technical departments such as ours.

The implication of that, my boss informed me, was that I had "hit the roof" in Stationery & Supplies department. My next promotion to a higher grade in the foreseeable future, he explained, could only be achieved outside Stationery & Supplies department.

"Are you prepared to move," he asked me. "Sure, if it is for progress, I am." I replied.

I was subsequently appointed Assistant Manager Communications Department in Head Office, Lagos, on a lateral transfer. Luckily for me, not long after that a general review of conditions of service of all Officers in the bank resulted to the movement of

every officer to his/her next grade above, in place of the usual incremental progression of one or more notches. That resulted to my elevation to officer Grade four (OG 4).

CONVERSION TO BRANCH BANKING OPERATIONS.

In Communications Department, part of my duties frequently brought me in contact with the Managing Director and Chief Executive Officer of the Bank, which exposed my level of performance on the job to his notice within a short time of my arrival in the Department. After I had completed a two-year stint in Communications Department, I might have made an impression in the mind of the Managing Director. One day, he initiated a discussion with me on the prospects of my converting to branch banking operations duty.

"What are you doing in Communications Department? Don't you think you are wasting your time there?" He asked. "I was transferred to the department sir," I replied.

"Don't you want to be a branch manager?" He asked, and added, "I am opening rural branches all over the place."

"I would like to be manager sir," I replied, "but I was employed as a secretarial staff and I have not undertaken any clerical branch operation duties since I joined the bank."

"Come off it my friend," he snapped back,

"you appear very intelligent, there is no magic about branch work, all you need is to be trained." he assured me.

While I was still in his office, I eavesdropped on his telephone conversation with the then Assistant General Manager (Staff).

".... I am convinced that he has capacity for more advanced work and I believe he is being under-utilized in Communications department. I want his talents tapped fully." he said.

"Transfer him to the office of the Area Manager, Lagos to undergo induction into branch management duties." The Managing Director concluded.

The Assistant General Manager (Staff) took his time, waited until I proceeded on my annual leave before he gave effect to that discussion.

I soon proceeded on my annual leave and while still on leave I received a letter from the Staff Manager saying, "Upon the expiration of your leave, would you please report to the Area Manager, Lagos for re-assignment." Initially, the instruction sounded vague to me and instead of reporting to the Area Manager, Lagos, I went to Head Office to obtain clarification of "re-assignment". It was verbally explained to me. That lateral move was again made in 1978 and a program for a twelve months induction at various branches within Lagos was arranged for me. The Area Manager, Lagos, told me he had been briefed on the conversation between the Managing Director and the Assistant General Manager (Staff) in respect of my conversion to branch operation duties.

The induction course was intended to be for one year but within six months, the Area Manager said that he was convinced that I could commence providing relief assignments for Accountants of small branches during annual leave periods.

"My boy," he said, "I think you should begin to take

responsibilities commensurate with your experience to be able to compete with the younger officers."

IN-SERVICE TRAINING.

To be fully equipped for the assignments of relieving Branch Accountants, however, I had to first attend an intensive in-service training in office administration at the Staff Training Center, Benin City, Bendel State, Nigeria. Thereafter, I undertook relief assignments for about one year, for Accountants of some of the small branches within Lagos as I continued to learn on the job.

The aim of the induction, I was made to understand, was specifically to prepare me for branch management duties. I was then nominated to attend another intensive "Branch Management Course," at the bank's Lagos Staff Training Center, Ebute Metta, Lagos. Prior to my nomination for the Branch Management Course, however, I was already holding a letter to go and relieve the Branch Accountant, Ebute Metta branch, Lagos at officer grade three (OG3) to allow her to proceed on annual leave.

That was to be my first actual upward movement in over six years largely because of my numerous lateral transfers during the period from Manager, Stationery & Supplies department to Assistant Manager, Communications and to branch operations induction. Remarkably, all those years, I earned double increments annually. By the bank's standard, that evidenced excellent performances which ordinarily should have attracted one or two promotions within the period.

I was privileged to attend the Branch Management Course and on the last day of the course, it was conventional for the participants to attend a cocktail party usually organized at the instance of the Executive Director (Staff), to create a forum for prospective Managers to ask questions about their career prospects in the bank. I considered the time opportune to ask the Executive Director (Staff) a question that touched on my career, and I did. "Sir, do you see anything wrong with a situation where an officer earned double increments for seven consecutive years in this bank and yet he did not earn promotion?" I asked him.

"That is an anomaly" he promptly answered.

"If any officer earns double increments in three consecutive years, he should be promoted." He explained.

"The officer did not have a warning letter?" He asked.

"No, never, not even a verbal warning sir," I answered.

"In that case, something may have gone wrong." he said,

"Who is this officer?" He asked, and I replied, it is I"

"My Principal Staff Officers will look at that first thing on Monday morning," he assured me.

"In the meantime, you may forward your letter of

complaint and address it directly to my office, without delay, if you feel strongly about the anomaly," he concluded.

I seized the opportunity to remind the Executive Director (Staff) that there might be other officers who, like me, could be suffering the same fate in silence scattered all over the bank's network of branches. Some of them might not have an opportunity to attend a management course to complain like I just did. He promised to investigate the whole matter of assessing all officers in the bank, which he did.

ACCELERATED PROMOTION/APPOINTMENT

Of course, I felt strongly about the anomaly and I submitted the letter of complaint as instructed by the Executive Director (Staff). I proceeded on my annual leave immediately after the Management Course. A few weeks  later, while I was still on vacation, I received a letter of accelerated promotion to Officer grade two (OG2), from officer grade four (OG 4), and in addition, appointed to act as Relief Manager within Lagos, instead of going to relieve Accountant (OG3) at Ebute Metta branch, upon my return from leave. A patient dog they say eats the fattest bone!

The acting period as Relief Manager was to be for six months but for some inexplicable reasons, to which I was not privy, it took twelve months for the confirmation to come through! The Relief Manager assignments, however, continued until 1984 when I was appointed substantive Assistant Manager, Abibu Oki Branch and promoted to officer grade one (OG 1). While serving at Abibu Oki Branch, I had the privilege first to provide relief for the Deputy Manager (SMP 5) and later to attend an external course - "Marketing of Financial Services" - at the Financial Institutions Training Center, Yaba, Lagos, Nigeria.

Four years later, I was promoted to senior management position six (SMP 6) and appointed Assistant Manager, Stock Exchange House Branch, the bank's corporate branch in Lagos. While there, I provided relief for the Manager, at (SMP4) soon after I reported at the branch to enable him to proceed on his annual leave. My stay at Stock Exchange House Branch was cut short by my temporary appointment as Manager, Ajegunle branch, Apapa, which in the assessment of the Assistant General Manager, (Lagos) had been inefficiently managed over a period and he needed a senior officer to "go and stay there until all the anomalies have been rectified."

After completing that assignment, I was nominated to attend "Managers' Advances" course, after which I was subsequently transferred to Head Office and appointed a Head Office Debt Recovery Manager with responsibility for Lagos Island, Edo, Delta and Niger States. As a Head Office debt recovery Manager, I was based in Lagos and only made trips to the other states periodically. I was not particularly happy with the assignment because I did not find it sufficiently challenging.

At that time, however, I was already qualified for my maximum retirement percentage benefits of one year's salary as gratuity and seventy percent of annual basic salary as monthly pension at thirty years' service. I felt it was time to move on after serving the bank for thirty-four years. The bank had over the years metamorphosed from Bank of West Africa Limited, when I was employed, to First Bank of Nigeria Plc. through name changes. I gave notice of one month of my intention to voluntarily retire.

On learning of my intention to retire, the Managing Director invited me to his office to ascertain that I was not leaving because the bank had earlier rejected my application for permission to accept a director position in a Community bank while still in the service of First Bank. I assured him that it

was not, but that I had to go since, in any event, if I stayed on, I would still have to proceed on compulsory retirement after thirty-five years' service – just one year later.

PREPARING FOR RETIREMENT

Was I fully prepared for retirement at the time I took the decision to retire from First Bank's service? At that time, I had thought I was, but in retrospect, knowing what I know now, "no, I wasn't."

At the time I gave notice of my intention to retire majority of my kids were just entering tertiary institutions. I had no substantial savings or investment, no business to retire to, and my only assured income after retirement was to be my meager pension, and irregular rents from two bungalows that I erected with a staff building loan obtained a few years back. I was still repaying the staff loan at the time, but I knew I had already served First Bank for a little over thirty-four years. Even if I had to wait for compulsory retirement age one year later, it would not still have made any difference because my percentage gratuity and pension would not have increased; I mandated deductions from my monthly pension as repayments. I was determined to spend the rest of my active years doing something new, even if I had not yet identified what that something new would be – a huge mistake that my readers must avoid!

However, if we put our faith in God, He never turns His back on us. Fortunately, in this instance, He made sure that when one road closed, another opened. It was divine providence therefore that at the time I was retiring from the services of First Bank, Irrua

Community Bank Nigeria Limited was also coming on stream. I understood that my income (pension and rent) would inevitably be significantly less after retiring from First Bank of Nigeria Limited.

"How could I possibly meet the educational needs of five kids in tertiary institutions, and one in an expensive secondary school, from a meager pension if I did not tag on to something with extra remuneration to supplement my pension and rent income?" I reasoned.

The good news was that as I was retiring from First Bank, I was literally being persuaded to accept an offer of a contract employment to help set up and manage the Community Bank. That offer of appointment came timely to shield what might probably have been an embarrassment resulting from my decision to retire without a definite plan. The benefit of the Community Bank appointment was that there would be no hustle for employment, no financial headache because I had my own house to live in, and no boredom – three things that might have combined to lead to frustration, depression, sickness and, possibly, early death.

AVOIDING UNNECESSARY EXPENDITURE

There is no alternative to a timely retirement plan. Financial security at old age must be put in the front burner while you are still young. You need to learn from the mistakes of those before you who have travelled the distance if you are to enjoy financial security in your retirement. A considerable amount of money would undoubtedly pass through your hands during your active life.

A good retirement starts on the day you receive your first pay check knowing that whatever has a beginning also has an end. Thirty-five or sixty years mandatory service are certainly not forever. Some experts say unless you tell every dollar what to do, you would later wonder where all the money went when you retire! One way of preparing for retirement therefore is careful planning while still in your active years. It would be foolhardy to wait until retirement is one, three or even five years away before you start planning for it.

I was discussing with a young lady recently and she said to me, "I don't think I want to buy a new car again or any car for that matter on mortgage." "Why?" I asked her.

"I once bought a brand-new car on which I spent nearly all the small savings I had put together over the years to pay the deposit, and for the next one year, the little money I could have been putting away as savings was going towards the payment of the monthly mortgage on the car. It was clear to me that I could not sustain that trend and make any savings." she replied.

"What did you do next?" I asked.

"Of course, I sold it to a dealership and got back as much money as I could to stop the "bleeding" on my monthly savings. I bought a good used car which I paid for in cash from the proceeds of sale of the new car and was left with a small balance which I put back into my savings." She replied.

"That's a very smart economic sense," I commended her.

Ordinarily, there is nothing wrong in buying a car or any other household appliance for that matter new if you can conveniently afford it, but if its acquisition could have the effect of interfering with your dedicated savings towards preparing early for retirement for instance, you need to give it a second thought before taking a plunge. Most used cars, particularly in the United States are generally reliable and their costs are so reasonable that you can conveniently obviate the luxury to buy a car new, if doing so can stagnate your early preparation for retirement.

We are all prone to make some unfavorable decisions at some point in our lives. The lesson to learn here is that you should not be afraid to reverse such decisions anytime you are convinced that you have made them. Most people stick with the effect of an unfavorable decision, even when they are affected negatively, because of their worry about the opinions of other people. It is

good to always remember that your real existence is in yourself and not in any other people's opinion. No one knows you better than you know yourself.

PLANNING FOR FINANCIAL SECURITY

For the sake of financial security, it is advisable for you to cultivate the habit of early preparation for retirement from when you secure your first employment. That goes for all young adults in paid or self-employment. Set up a savings or any other investment and religiously fund it monthly unfailingly. Never look the way of that account when you need money, unless to invest, until retirement age. If you religiously fund that account for thirty-five years, assuming you remain in paid employment, no matter how little that amount would be, it could make you a millionaire by the time you are ready to retire. That can give you a measure of financial security, even if nothing else comes up. With present day technology, and availability of numerous books and electronic teachings on preparing early for retirement, nobody should have any excuse for inadequate financial preparation for retirement, which you know from day one must come sooner or later.

Retirement from active service is not a reward for what we have done. Like old age, it is a special gift from God. Some people go into it and die within a short time, others live through it for a very long time in good health. Through the Grace of God, I have so far enjoyed a retired life for over twenty-five years but had remained actively engaged for fifteen out of the twenty-five years. The financial preparation for retirement apart, no matter who we are, retirement presents us with two choices. Either we can use it for self-indulgence or we can use it to make an impact on the lives of others; the choice we face is between empty self-indulgence and meaningful activity.

While still in your active years of service, it is not uncommon to wish you were already due for retirement, but at the time retirement stares you in the face, you might find yourself asking, "Am I ready? Have I prepared adequately? what do I do with my time upon retirement?" and "where do I go to every day?"

Unless you have a definite plan for life after retirement, the first few weeks and months could be both challenging and sometimes boring; therefore, it is imperative that you work out whatever alternatives you have in place before the time arrives. The important thing is that while you are working out the details, you already have the financial buffer you might have built over many years through careful planning that could have the effect of at least providing financial stability for you and your family.

Retirement from whatever you are doing might be one of the most important decisions you would make in your life because it affects you, your spouse and your entire family. Before you take the decision, consider your situation, discuss with your spouse and give a thought to the pitfalls and the inevitable changes that retirement would bring to your entire life, your spouse and all those who look up to you for their sustenance.

That could obviate the necessity to feel inadequate and depressed later. Some people give in to illness because of inadequate preparation and die very early in their retirement life.

REASONS FOR RETIREMENT

There is a multiplicity of reasons why people retire though, and not everybody who retired did so for reasons of old age or length of service. Some retired to change working or living environment, some to set up new businesses, some because of health concerns and a host of other reasons, but the ultimate retirement in focus here is one due to declining productivity arising from old age, length of service or infirmity. Whatever your own reasons are, the most important consideration should be adequate preparation for what you are about to do, and it must start early.

It is important therefore to ascertain that you are ready physically, emotionally, financially and that those who will be affected by the overall consequences of your decision are given the opportunity of an input for the overall benefit of members of your family. Otherwise it could be challenging if it becomes compulsory that you must retire, even when you have not planned for it. It is advantageous to plan towards achieving voluntary retirement instead of waiting for a compulsory one. Once you have done your due diligence and you faithfully place your trust in God, everything else would fall in place for your overall happiness. It is only by placing God at the center of everything you do that you can make sense out of life.

CHAPTER 6

MANAGING A COMMUNITY BANK.

Without my prior knowledge, while my notice of retirement from First Bank was running, a Community Bank was in the process of being established in my town. I subsequently subscribed to the ordinary shares and was offered a position on the board as a director. My application to my employers, First Bank, for permission to accept the offer was turned down as a rule. While that was on, my colleagues on the Community Bank board got together and requested the Chairman to discuss with me the possibility of my assisting with establishing the bank and managing it. My acceptance they reasoned would obviate the necessity to search for another manager, since I had given notice of retirement from the services of First Bank and I had plans to relocate to my town.

Considering the initial inevitable void assisting to establish and manage the Community Bank could fill, coming so soon after my retirement, I pondered on the initiative and graciously accepted the offer on a renewable contract basis for the first five years. I thus became a director in and the pioneer manager of the new Community Bank. It was commissioned on February 21, 1992 and business commenced on the same day. A lot of work had to be undertaken for the bank to have a foothold in the town and get the inhabitants to imbibe the habit of saving money in a bank.

A few years down the road, the Community Banks

supervisory body, modified some of the original concepts of community banking. One of the innovations to the Community banking system was the abolition of director/manager position perhaps because of perceived operational conflicts. The implication was that you could either be a Director or a Manager, not both. Considering the impact that managing the Community Bank was already making in the community, I opted to resign from the board and continued as the manager since it would be easier to replace me as a director.

Community banking was introduced by government principally for the benefit of the small-scale business operators, particularly in the rural areas who could not easily access loan facilities from the commercial and merchant banks because of collateral requirements. However, to offer the same opportunities to small scale entrepreneurs based in urban areas, licensing of community banks was not restricted to rural areas only. The initial minimum capital requirement was two hundred and fifty thousand naira only. Perhaps, because of observed inadequacies after the introduction, the minimum paid up capital was progressively increased until it reached a point where it overwhelmed many of the already functioning licensed Community banks, particularly when the minimum Paid Up capital was raised to N20m. (twenty million naira) from N5m (five million naira!)

I experienced a checkered history during the fifteen years that I managed the Community bank with strange occurrences that I did not experience in my over thirty-four years working in First Bank in Lagos.

1). The date was January 23, 1993 and the time was 1.30 pm. less than one year after the commissioning of the bank. My destination was Lagos, Nigeria, and accompanying me on the trip was my younger brother, Godwin, and another young lady (I cannot remember her name now). Soon after driving through Benin City, Edo State in Nigeria, a few hundred yards to River Ovia along Benin-Lagos Expressway, the official vehicle in which I was travelling to invest some of the bank's excess funds, was just gathering momentum. We were beginning to cruise at a speed of about eighty kilometers per hour. Then I heard a loud sound and my vehicle wobbled. I knew it was the sound of a burst tire.

"Don't step on the brake, just control the vehicle." I immediately admonished the driver. "Okay sir" he promptly replied.

Not only did the driver step on the brake, but from my sitting position I could see him press down on the pedal completely, (I guess he had panicked) and once the front wheels got locked at that speed, the vehicle took off, somersaulted three times and "bang!" it landed on its roof and finally its right side before it came to a stop. All four of us were still inside the vehicle but the wind screens and all the side glasses were either broken or ripped off. Luckily for us, no other vehicle was close to us in front and at the back when the accident occurred.

I quickly listened to my body but did not feel any pain. Then I looked at my younger brother who sat beside me in the vehicle; I saw his head droop and rested on the headrest of the driver's seat. He was bleeding from one finger of his right hand. "Godwin", I called his name.

Apparently not conscious, he did not respond. I quickly carried him out of the car myself. I was frightened and, still holding him in my arms, I looked up to God and prayed, "O'God, don't let him die." Suddenly my brother jerked back to consciousness right in my arms! It was unbelievable.

"Wao! This is prayer answered instantly." I conjectured, then, silently I said, "Lord, I thank you." Like somebody suddenly woken from sleep, my brother asked, "what happened." "Don't worry, we just had a lone accident, please sit down." I said to him.

The driver had hit his chest against the steering wheel because he refused to make use of the seat belt. He was stretchered out by the road side and was in pains. I was also worried about him.

"Are you okay?" I asked him, but his only answer was a gesticulation.

As a large crowd of sympathizers gathered, and some other drivers sped past the scene, God sent one "good Samaritan" who kindly offered to drive us all in his pick-up van to the ER of the University Teaching Hospital,

(UBTH) Benin City, for examination and possible treatment. Luckily the hospital was not far away; on arrival I asked the "good Samaritan" who kindly helped us.

"How much do I owe you?"

"Nothing sir," he replied, "I just helped you."

As he drove away, I kept praying for him until his vehicle disappeared from my sight. We spent the rest of the day and one night in the hospital before we were discharged the following morning. Miraculously, through the Grace of God I was again not hurt in that accident. Like the first one I had in Onitsha in 1966, I did not even suffer any shock, but the vehicle was a write-off.

I imagined myself - almost six feet frame inside the mangled wreckage of the vehicle as it somersaulted repeatedly - escape unhurt from such a terrible accident and I gave thanks to the Almighty God. The Peugeot 504 Estate was a complete wreck and was later to be auctioned for only N12,000.00! Despite being in a rural town, when the bank was commissioned, it had a very good start-up in the early years, posting good annual results which enabled the directors to recommend the issue of bonus shares to shareholders to meet the progressively increasing minimum paid up capital. There was therefore no necessity to call on them to inject their funds. Between 1992 and 2004, it was increased to three million naira and later to five million naira. A substantial proportion of the increased share capitals were met from reserves previously posted from profits by the bank. That was despite the unexpected losses arising from armed robberies the bank suffered within that period amounting to a total of over one million, three hundred thousand naira on two separate occasions.

MENACE OF MEN OF THE UNDERWORLD

In all my thirty-four years' service with First Bank I did not witness or experience any armed robbery, neither did I have cause to make a statement to the police about one, not even for fraud.

2). The first sad experience I had with men of the underworld in the Community Bank was the theft of the Manager's official vehicle from my secured premises on a night a World Cup soccer match (USA '94) involving Nigeria was played. The match extended till late into the night and many soccer fans had come to watch on television at my house; it lasted till about two o'clock a.m. When the match ended, because it was rather late, all the fans slept in my house. In the morning when the driver came to ask for the car key, my nephew-in-law knocked at my door and asked,

"sir, where is the car? The driver wants to wash it."

"It is parked in the usual place." I replied.

"But sir, the car is not there, did you take it out last night?" the youngman asked me.

Surprised at the question, I accompanied him to where

the vehicle was usually parked; it was not there. A close observation revealed a Master Key on the ground where I had personally parked the car, and I remembered that I had activated the fuel cut security system.

"The car must have been stolen overnight either while we were watching football or while I was asleep," I concluded, and went on to check the metal gate. There was evidence that the padlock had also been damaged; a confirmation that something ominous had happened.

"They cannot go very far, I activated the fuel cut security yesterday when I parked the vehicle." I assured the driver.

We then took my personal car and drove around in the hope of finding the bank's vehicle abandoned somewhere around the vicinity (because of the fuel cut system). As we drove close to eleven miles on the road to Benin, I told the driver to stop the car.

"If the vehicle could get this far without the fuel supply cutting, then the thieves must have found a solution to the fuel cut security. Let's go and make a report of the theft to the police." I told him.

The matter was reported to the Police and radio messages were sent to all the Police formations in Edo State. All efforts to trace the vehicle were unsuccessful. At the time of the theft we had recently spent a substantial amount of money to refurbish the vehicle. About four months later, it was recovered in Kaduna State, Northern Nigeria by a Police Officer from Benin

City, Edo State who had gone there to investigate the theft of another vehicle. The plate number of our vehicle was discovered to have been changed and a panel beater was in the process of also changing the windscreens and all the glasses because they were engraved with the original vehicle number.

When we retrieved the vehicle from Kaduna State with the help of the cops, it was found to have been massively vandalized. The new alternator, battery, five new tires and many other accessories had been removed and replaced with old ones. The vehicle was in a deplorable state. It was put back in a roadworthy condition at a cost of almost another one hundred thousand naira. I was amazed how the vehicle got to Kaduna. For somebody to have successfully stolen a vehicle parked at the back of a secured premises with two locked metal gates, I believed that thief must be somebody who was very familiar with the environment – but whoever the thief was, he was never traced.

FIRST ARMED ATTACK

3) Unknown to me, that theft was only a tip of the iceberg. Within one year of the recovery of the bank's vehicle, an armed robbery attack on the bank itself took place on a Friday night in the 'ember months of 1995. The criminals came in the middle of the night when only the two unarmed bank security guards were on duty. The robbers tied them up before forcing their way

through the main entrance door and broke into the strong room. It must be said that the Strong room was not a standard one because it did not have a grill gate and door, but just a locally fabricated metal door and a metal protector. That was because nobody envisaged at the onset that any group of criminals would contemplate taking up arms against such small outfits. The armed robbers subsequently did, and they might have accessed the cheap overnight cash safe with the aid of a chisel and sledgehammer; they virtually emptied its contents. Nearly one-million-naira cash was lost to them on that night, which for a rural community bank at that time was substantial being almost double the bank's total paid up capital. The Bank was forced to close its doors to business while I did what was humanly possible to ensure the replacement of the damaged overnight cash Safe with a solid fireproof one. Within two weeks, the bank reopened for business.

SECOND ARMED ATTACK

4). The second armed robbery attack was more traumatic. The time was just before nine o'clock in the morning soon after the bank opened for the day's business. I had hardly settled into my office when I heard a voice asking, "where is the cash?"

Thinking that the voice was coming from one humorous customer, unruffled, I answered without raising up my head.

"This is manager's office, we don't keep cash here." I said.

When I looked up, already standing in front of me was a strange unmasked young man, perhaps in his early twenties. Clutching a pump action weapon and, pointing it to my forehead, he thundered,

"where is the key to the strong room?"

I frantically jumped to my feet and placed both hands on top of my desk – to indicate no tricks. My instinct immediately told me he might be on drugs and could pull the trigger for no reason! Still unruffled, I answered quickly,

"The Accountant holds the key."

With the weapon still pointed at my head, the young man went behind my back, got hold of the belt on my pants and, without saying a word, he pushed me through the side door leading to the banking hall.

"How much closer to death could I have come?" I sighed! Then it dawned on me, after over thirty-eight years of working in banking environments, that there was no profession without its own hazards!

When I entered the banking hall, I was astounded to discover that all the staff and customers had surrendered to another member of this armed gang who was also brandishing another automatic weapon; everybody - staff and customers alike - laid on the floor, face down in absolute silence. Yet another ransacked the cashiers' cubicles for cash. None of them was masked and three of them were inside the bank. I was to learn later that one had taken position outside while the fifth one was inside a car parked along the road with its engine running.

"How much money did an armed robber expect to find in a rural Community Bank for him to risk possible arrest or even shot if caught?" I wondered instinctively.

"Where is the key?" The robber asked again. "Don't waste my time!"

I quickly called the Accountant who rose from the floor and he called the second key holder who also rose. Without saying anything to me or to anyone else, the armed man then left me and led them both to the "strong room".

Knowing that it could be risky for me to try to return to my office under the prevailing circumstances, I found a space and laid face down in the banking hall. The invaders collected all the cash they could find in the safe and in the cashiers' cubicles unchallenged. About five hundred thousand naira was again taken away in addition to the cash they also collected from some customers who were waiting at the counter to lodge money into their accounts. All the money was loaded in what is popularly known in Nigeria as Ghana must Go bags and in a commando style, one of them, presumably their leader, shouted an order, "let's go!"

They quietly left without firing a single shot because we gave them no reasons so to do.

What baffled everyone around was the fact that the robbers did not operate like a group that expected a challenge throughout. They appeared to be in no hurry, as one would have expected, to rob and leave the scene quickly. Clutching the bags with the bank's money they jumped into the waiting car parked along the road and zoomed off. As we heard the screeching sound of their car tires, we tried to get up from our prostrate positions, believing they had gone. Suddenly, the sound of a gunshot was heard, and everybody went down again.

"Police," a loud voice said.

Behold, it was the armed policeman in mufti supposedly on bank guard.

"Where have you been?" I asked him.

"When I saw the robbers enter the bank," he said, "I decided to go into hiding because I was only in possession of a pistol which I know was not a match for the automatic weapons the armed robbers carried." He replied.

An armed policeman saw robbers enter a bank he was supposed to be guarding and hid for over thirty minutes (outside the Bank premises) without doing anything – not even to call for reinforcement from the station less than one hundred & fifty yards away – and he reappeared casually with a gunshot into the air after the robbery! It was disgusting.

It's been almost twenty-three years now and I suppose it was about time one aired one's views about that robbery incident. To this day, the scenario left a bad impression on the minds of many people and a sour taste in the mouth. It may never be known because of the coincidences, whether those who manned the Law Enforcement outfit in the town at the time were just downright incompetent, scared, or at worst, nonchalant in that encounter.

For instance, it was reliably learned soon after the robbery operation, that the Acting Head of the Security outfit, whose station by the way was less than one hundred and fifty yards away from the bank along the same road, was informed of the robbery incident in good time for his men to have shown up at the scene while the robbers were still operating. They, the robbers, must have spent more than thirty minutes in the bank without exhibiting any signs of anxiety or urgency. They carried on like a team doing a legitimate job. There were no GSM phones then and they did not even bother to disable the land telephone line!

Surprisingly, within about three minutes of the Police officer on bank guard duty firing a gun-shot into the air, and he announced his presence, the Acting Head of the security outfit showed up at the bank accompanied by a team of his armed men, an action which could be likened to rushing to shut the gate after the horse had left the stable! While everyone was still in shock and apprehension over what just took place, the Security chief frantically asked me,

"Where are they? Which way did they go?" and without waiting for an answer, he volunteered,
"we were looking for the key to the armory!!"
"Seriously?" I took a hard look at him and repeated in my head,
"looking for the key to the armory!"
I was shocked and became skeptical about the credibility of that claim. His own demeanor, and the body language of his gun tottering personnel were akin to an act in a Nollywood movie. They then drove off and returned less than ten minutes later.
"How much did they take?" The officer asked me.
"How am I supposed to know how much they took so soon after such a traumatic experience?" I asked him.
"We have not even entered the strong room." I reminded him.
"It's just because I need to know," the officer added.
I was confused because I did not get it. How could knowing the amount the robbers took take precedence over the need to urgently attempt to go after and possibly apprehend them at that stage? He said no more, did nothing else and without entering the bank for on the spot assessment, he drove away, accompanied by all his armed men.
The questions that readily troubled my mind at that point and to which I could not find answers were: -
"How did the officer on bank guard recognize the robbers as they entered into the bank?" Surely their

weapons must have been concealed until they were inside the bank.

"why did he do nothing in over thirty minutes other than hide until he knew the robbers had left?

" what was the necessity for him to fire a shot into the air before he came into the bank?" The robbers had left! Was it to scare the already traumatized staff and customers or to indicate to somebody elsewhere that the robbers had gone?

"Why did the team of armed police arrive within only a few minutes after the gun-shot sound when, in fact, they had been alerted by a third party almost thirty minutes before?"

"How couldn't somebody in the station know where the key to the armory was kept for such a long time? Was there nobody in charge of such an important section?"

What if it was the police station that was under attack, what would the Police authorities have done in such a situation where nobody knew the whereabouts of the key to the armory?"

There were more questions than answers; all the stories surrounding the delayed response were difficult to piece together.

The entire scenario did not make much sense to me, but since they were the only ones we relied on for protection, I considered that silence was golden at that stage while we let them do their work. Just as I suspected, the investigation of that case, if there was any, like the previous robbery, never got off the ground and the matter died a natural death.

THIRD ARMED ATTACK- REPELLED

5). A third attempt was made, also at night a few years later, but the armed policemen on night guard repelled that attack as the robbers tried to lock them inside the bank's security guard post. One of the robbers was alleged to have escaped with bullet wounds, leaving blood stains on the bank's Security post door after the police shot through it, evidencing that claim. Overall, my joy was that we were able to manage all the above scary scenarios in such manner that apart from losing cash, nobody took a bullet, and no life was wasted.

A few of the community banks, at least, in Esan, Edo State of Nigeria, particularly in the rural communities became vulnerable to armed robberies and were in fact similarly attacked once the criminals knew that the capital base of each bank was insufficient to enable it to acquire a solid fireproof overnight cash safe. Apart from our Community Bank, two sister Community Banks, in two neighboring towns were similar victims of armed robbery attacks at different times.

MIGRATION TO MICRO FINANCE BANKS

Perhaps, to mitigate the above scenario, the minimum capital base of all the operating Community Banks was increased from five million naira to twenty million naira with a view to their migrating to a new concept - Micro Finance Banking system – not later than the end of November 2007. Once the information was in the public domain, expectedly, deposits from fringe customers virtually stopped, and customers commenced large scale panic withdrawal of their funds. Similarly, most dishonest borrowing customers either slowed down on repayments or stopped servicing their facilities in anticipation of the deadline. There was a run and unfortunately, many of the banks, including our Community Bank, could not raise the twenty million naira minimum paid up capital by the deadline. Those banks that met the new minimum paid up capital migrated to Micro Finance Banks while all others ceased to exist even as Community Banks and were obliged to close shop.

THEFT OF COMPUTER HARDWARE

. 6) At some point in the existence of our Community Bank, manual banking work was becoming too laborious because of the level of patronage and the board of directors decided to computerize its operations. The computer software and hardware had been procured at a cost of over one million naira, and we were in the middle of computerizing our operations. This exercise could not be completed when the bank was obliged to close shop in 2007. All the desktop monitors, the server and other computer hardware were kept in the bank building. A break-in through one of the windows at a time the bank was no longer in operation again took place early in 2009 and all the new desktop monitors including the Server were stolen and the incident was reported to the Police for investigation. Nothing further was heard.

During the fifteen years the bank operated, the town, especially the metropolis, witnessed tremendous rise in commercial activities. For instance, prior to the commissioning of the bank, virtually all the lock up stores were under lock and key because of commercial inactivity. The Community Bank engendered awareness in commerce and agriculture and encouraged farmers, traders and other entrepreneurs with banking facilities, a phenomenon which attracted customers even from neighboring towns with Community and Commercial banking facilities too, to open accounts with our bank.

As at the time the Community Bank was obliged to close shop at the end of 2007, it was difficult to find stores to rent in the town because of the awareness engendered by the bank which led to increased commercial activity. The situation was such that the few owners of business concerns in the town had to resort to leasing land and erecting their own buildings to meet their new expansion needs.

The Bank had on its pay roll a total of twenty-three staff members at the time it closed shop, most of who found themselves back in the labor market. I had already planned to severe my services at my age seventy years but was obliged to wait one more year in anticipation of the bank being able to raise the new capital and migrate to a Micro Finance Bank in 2007 before leaving. That was not to be.

CHAPTER 7

RAISING A FAMILY

Raising a family of my own and especially having kids had always been my desire because of my love for children. A few years after I secured a stable employment with Bank of West Africa Limited, I started to toy with the idea of getting married. Living within proximity at Griffith Street, Lagos brought Grace and I together in 1961 and we became friends, but even before we got to know ourselves well enough to discuss about a serious relationship, she became pregnant. Unfortunately, she lost that pregnancy a few months later and the doctor told us it was a set of twins. That did not break our friendship.

As if God was saying something to us, Grace became pregnant again within a few months. Nine months down the road she went into labor and I walked her to Island Maternity Hospital, Lagos, Nigeria, where she had registered for and received ante natal care all through the pregnancy. She was taken in and I returned home since it was not the norm then in that part of the world for a man to stay with his wife in the labor room. Hours later, I went back to the hospital to check if the baby had arrived and what I heard from the front desk staff shocked me.

"Congratulations," she said, and added, "she has given birth to twins, girls, alive."

I noticed that she was reading from a register. I looked back to check if she was talking to someone else, but I discovered that I was the only one standing with her.

"Did you say twins"? I asked curiously. "Yes, two girls." she answered. "A set of twins again."

I soliloquized instinctively and as I quietly walked away from her, the word "twins" continued to reverberate in my head – Grace miscarried a set of twins a little over a year ago! It did not quite register.

It sounded strange to me not because I was unhappy but because throughout the pregnancy and visits to the ante natal clinic, no nurse or doctor ever told us the sex of the baby, let alone how many we were expecting! We had prepared our minds and planned for one baby. So, rather than be excited at becoming a father and rush upstairs to see Grace and the babies, without saying one more word to the front desk staff, I staggered back home in confusion, pondering over how we could raise two baby girls, for whom we had not prepared, and at the same time. It must have been about an hour later before I regained composure in the house and I reconciled myself with the fact that God had just blessed us with two adorable kids. I became excited, but did I bargain for two?

"Grace must be wondering why I have not come back to see them." I reasoned. I rushed back to the hospital. I had no access to telephone facility then and indeed, Grace was wondering why I had not come to see her and the babies. They were doing okay, and she informed me that even the labor ward nurses did not know that they were taking delivery of twins until after the first baby girl was born.

"The age gap separating the two babies", she said "was only about ten minutes." As I looked over the crib I could see our two kids - the first I had brought to this world. My confusion gave way to excitement as I watched the innocent children, eyes closed and perhaps sleeping.

"Congratulations and thank you," I said to Grace. "You have made me a father."

One thing I did not have the courage to tell her was that I had come to the hospital earlier but went away in confusion when I was told she gave birth to twins; and I never did.

"How do people raise twins? I hear it is difficult. Are we going to be able to raise two baby girls at the same time?" I asked Grace. "Don't worry," she said, smiling.

"My immediate younger brothers are twins; my mother will help us." She assured me, perhaps, to allay what looked like my apprehension.

At the time Grace and I first met, she lived with her mother and several of her siblings in one room at Griffith Street, Lagos, next door to where I once lived. On arrival of the twin baby girls, it dawned on me that the atmosphere in that kind of setting would not be conducive for the healthy upbringing of our two bunches of joy, my first. Grace and I decided that as soon as they were discharged from the maternity ward, they would move in with me at Evans Street, a five minutes walking distance from Griffith where her mother lived, and they did just that.

It was just as well because still basking in the euphoria of becoming a dad, I could not have permitted the kids out of my sight. We named them Gladys and Gertrude. As the saying goes, the first love of a girl is her dad; My excitement was such that as soon as they were strong enough, I took our adorable babies to just about everywhere I went in the neighborhood as if to show them off to the world. Even without owning a car, I would rush home from work at lunch time not because I was hungry but just to be with Grace and play with our kids.

For the next few years we lived happily together while Grace and I continued to get to know each other better. Unfortunately, after the euphoria of being blessed with a set of twins wore out, Grace and I started to have misunderstandings which later snowballed to irreconcilable differences. We tried hard to salvage the relationship but due perhaps to inexperience, we failed. By mutual consent, Grace had to move out in January 1967, taking the kids with her. For the first few weeks I felt empty not seeing our kids because she took them far away and tried to deny me access to them.

Soon, Gladys and Gertrude were six years old and, luckily for me, they were registered in a school not far from where I lived on the Lagos Island. That made it possible for me to see the kids at school uninhibited.

After their sixth birthday, I pondered over the environment in which Gladys and Gertrude were being raised. Grace had left the kids under the care of their grandmother who lived alone. I tried to discuss with her the need to let the kids come and live with me if there was any reason why they could not live with her. Try as I did, she refused to cooperate. I exhausted all the options open to me for a mutually acceptable arrangement and we were not reaching any compromise. Much against my wish, unfortunately, I was left with no option than to seek the intervention of the social welfare department. After a protracted back and forth conversation midwifed by the department, what looked like an amicable solution was at last worked out taking the children's interest into account.

CHALLENGE OF CHILD CARE/ EVENTUAL MARRIAGE.

I had brought my younger sister Roseline in to take care of Gladys and Gertrude as an interim measure, but I knew from the onset that was temporary because she too would soon get married and leave us. Then the children would still need a mother figure; I decided that it was time to get married but I was not in any relationship.

Christiana was only fourteen years old in 1964 when she accompanied me to Lagos from Irrua, to join her elder sister who then just gave birth to her first baby girl. While we waited to board a vehicle to take us to Lagos, after my leave, my father, standing by me, took a good look at Christiana and jokingly asked her mother humorously: -

"Are you sure that this beautiful girl is not going to be my wife"?

My father still had two unmarried sons at the time, but he did not indicate who of his children he had in mind as potential suitor to the girl, and none of us bothered to ask that question. We all took it for a joke, laughed it away and nobody gave it any serious thought, since I already had Grace living with me.

Later in 1967 - long after Grace moved out of the house, Christiana, then over eighteen years old, was blossoming into a young woman. Determined not to remain single any longer and having no serious relationship at the time, I developed a soft spot for her. We became friends and later fell in love. Christiana was young and innocent, and I am not ashamed to say that our love started from the kitchen; but that is a story for another day and another book if God gives me the grace to live long enough to write another one. I continued to visit Christiana at her sister's house and it did not take very long before I proposed to her and she said, "yes." We had both discussed about the welfare of Gladys and Gertrude, and she had promised to shower them with motherly love. One thing led to another and by November of 1968, we got married under native law and custom and she moved in with us.

Incidentally, at the time I developed interest in Christiana, I had completely forgotten what transpired four years earlier until I broke the news of my interest in her to my father.

"Son, do you remember what I said to her mother four years ago?" he asked.

"Ah! yes dad, I remember now" I answered.

"Go ahead," he said to me, "you have my blessing; we know the family well."

What he jokingly said then turned out to be a prophesy that came to pass four years later.

When Christiana arrived in Lagos in 1964, Gladys and Gertrude were already two years old and she became acquainted with them because I had always visited her sister's house in the company of the kids even before Christiana came to Lagos. When we got married and she moved in with us, they were no strangers and she got on very well with the kids. That wiped away my fears of how they would relate as step mother and step daughters in the evolving circumstances. We lived happily together and exactly one year after, our first son, Gregory arrived precisely on November 6, 1969. Christiana had herself become a biological mother and continued to show motherly love and care to all three kids as her own. God subsequently blessed us with five other kids and as Christiana grew in experience and maturity, she also developed to be a loving wife to me and a caring mother to all the children.

Altogether, our family was blessed with eight children, three boys – Gregory, George, and Godfrey, and five girls - Gladys, Gertrude, Gillian, Gloria and Georgina. Christiana and I had put in every possible effort to shower all the eight kids with love up to when I voluntarily retired from the services of First Bank of Nigeria Limited in January 1992. To God be the Glory, except for Gregory (whose sun unfortunately set in October 2017), all our children are now grown up men and women striving hard to hold their own in different spheres of life in various parts of the world.

Up until the day my wife Christiana (of blessed memory) suddenly transited to Glory in 2002, not many of our friends knew that not all the kids were her biological children because of the way that she raised all of them. Through some of them, by the Grace of God, we have to date already been blessed with twenty-three grandchildren so far, still counting. My wife and I had earlier discussed the issue of retirement and we agreed that Godfrey, our youngest son, who then had just been admitted into Saint Finbarr's' Secondary school Akoka in Lagos, should be allowed to complete his first academic year to avoid his losing one school year. I left my wife behind in Lagos as a result for the rest of that academic year.

While in Irrua, I secured admission for Godfrey at Lumen Christi Catholic College, Uromi, and rented a store which I renovated as a hair dressing salon in Irrua for Christiana; she was a hair dresser and cosmetologist. They both joined me after nine months at a time all our other kids had secured admission into tertiary institutions, except for Gladys and Gertrude, who were already in paid employments. With a home of our own and the Irrua Community Bank Nigeria Limited job available after I retired voluntarily from First Bank of Nigeria Plc., settling down in Irrua did not present any problems for any of the three of us. We were happy; Christiana and I started to renew our old friendships, where they still existed, while initiating new ones in our home environment where we both grew up and had left many years before.

UNIQUE WEDDING OF TWO DAUGHTERS.

Our fourth daughter, Obehiaye Gloria graduated from University of Lagos while our fifth daughter, Isedua Georgina graduated from Auchi Polytechnic, Edo State in Nigeria. The two girls had attended the same primary school in Lagos, and they both also went on to complete their secondary school education at Federal Government Girls' College, Bida, in Niger State. After completing their first-degree education, they had separately introduced to us their suitors. Soon after her National Youth Service in 1998, Gloria had travelled to the United States of America, and Georgina returned home to live with us in Irrua on completion of her own Youth Service two years later, ready for employment.

By coincidence, through parental interaction, we had found out that both kids were separately nursing the idea of marriage in the second half of the same year. While, as parents, Christiana and I were not averse to the fulfilment of our kids' hearts desires, we thought of the financial burden of pulling off two weddings at such short interval. After separate discussions with them, Christiana and I toyed with the idea of a possible joint wedding with a view to minimizing cost. But as I had never known of two sisters' wedding on the same day, we consulted with the Parish Administrator of our church and were relieved to know that the Catholic Church had nothing against such an arrangement. The wedding date for both was then fixed for December 16, 2000.

The Traditional Marriage Ceremony dates then posed another challenge. While Gloria's suitor, Shola's family members, were to travel from Lagos State, the family members of Ese, Georgina's suitor were to travel from Sapele, Delta State. Traditional Marriage being predominantly a family affair, and its time-consuming process in our part of the world, we found it practically impossible to host the two families on the same day in our home without undue inconvenience, as we could do with the church wedding.

The dates were then staggered between the last two week-ends immediately prior to the wedding date, December 16, 2000. After fulfilling separately, the traditional marriage ceremony requirements, Gloria and Georgina later had an elaborate wedding ceremony and, as the saying goes, we the parents had "used one stone to kill two birds!" It turned out to be a historic event for my family, the Annunciation Catholic Church, Irrua, and our community, Esan in Edo State. Both Gloria and Georgina currently live happily in the United States with their spouses, (who coincidently are now pastoring two different churches), and their kids.

THE TRAGIC HOME CALL OF CHRISTIANA

Christiana had enjoyed excellent health since we got married and, although she did not have a medical training background, I'd come to depend on her proficient handling of the  minor health issues in our home. Ironically, in the first week of November 2002, she herself complained to me of ill-health and general body weakness; hitherto, because Christiana was a very strong and active person, she was very rarely sick. She was not the kind of person who bothered anyone, least of all her husband, with little things she could handle. So, anytime she told me she was sick, I fretted because I would know that it was more than just indisposition. I was to find out that she had gone to see a doctor twice within that week at the Specialist Teaching Hospital near our home and, curiously, on both occasions, her blood pressure reading had risen above her normal; but, might be because she was given medication, she did not even tell me about it.

Unlike me, Christiana had never been known to be hypertensive and had never been placed on any high blood pressure control medication. She was generally healthy.

"Why then should her reading be high?" My mind was agitated.

"What happened?" I had no clue whatsoever.

Even at that, there appeared to be nothing to indicate that her condition was so serious as to generate any anxiety. Nevertheless, as if I had a premonition, I promised that I would accompany her on the next doctor's appointment. *I wish I knew then that the next doctor's appointment was going to be to rush her to the ER in less than another thirty minutes that same day!*

After having a conversation that morning, I went into the kitchen to squeeze out a cup of fresh orange juice for my wife, but when I returned to the children's room where we had a conversation, she was no longer there. I went to our bedroom, but I did not see her on the bed either as I expected. As I turned to leave, wondering where she could be, I heard her voice on the floor near the door to the bathroom attached to our bedroom.

"Papa Greg," as she often called me, "help me."

My wife had slumped! The glass of juice I was holding almost fell from my hand as I rushed to pick her up.

"What happened, did you trip?" I asked her.

"I feel like throwing up," was her only reply.

A bowl of water was rushed in by our son, Godfrey, who had come from the university campus to visit. Possibly, because she had not eaten anything that morning, all she threw up was some watery substance. I still did not know the enormity of the problem I had in my hands until I asked her again;

"Did you hit your head against anything as you went down?"

she gesticulated 'no' by shaking her head.

Three times she took water from the bowl in my hands and washed her face by herself, while sitting with me on the bed.

While I sent for the doctor who was our tenant and worked with Irrua Specialist Teaching hospital, Christiana said in a somewhat slur tone,

"It's like my fingers are numb."

I became frightened, quickly grabbed the car keys and assisted by the doctor, I helped her into the car. Accompanied by the bank's driver who happened to be my wife's nephew, we were in the hospital in less than ten minutes. By the time we arrived at the hospital, I was shocked to find out that my wife had gone into a coma – just like that; a woman who was talking with me fifteen minutes before! I could not understand what was happening.

While doctors battled to resuscitate my wife and save her life, I rushed to the Parish Administrator's house just in case. While I was waiting to see him, the Assistant Parish Administrator showed up and on learning of my wife's condition, he accompanied me to the hospital. It was a miracle that I remembered to do that considering my level of anxiety over Christiana's condition. By the time I returned, she had been placed on oxygen. Throughout our stay at the hospital, the only time I saw her move any of her limbs was when the priest sprinkled Holy Water on her beautiful face. With her eyes still closed, she moved her head a little and I saw a mild smile on her lips like acknowledging the Holy Water. I was moved with trepidation which almost forced tears from my eyes. That gave me a false hope that she would eventually make it out of the coma. How wrong I was, she never did.

Because Christiana had never been that sick before, I quickly informed all our kids and urged them to pray for their mom. To date, that night remains my longest night ever. I had left the hospital in the wee hours of that night to check on our two years old grandson,

Ehimare, and to bring new clothes for Christiana to change into in the morning. Then suddenly, at about six o'clock in the morning, I heard the screams of the young lady whom I had left in the hospital with my wife.

"Daddy! Daddy," she screamed "come o, they say her condition has changed."

"Changed for the better or worse?" I conjectured.

The fear that penetrated me was colder than ice, and I pondered madly over the events of the less than twenty-four hours or so as I hurried back to the hospital. My heart skipped beats while my subconscious mind kept telling me that the worst had happened. Indeed, it had and there on the hospital bed Christiana laid quietly as if she was sleeping. I frantically broke through the cordon of sympathetic nurses surrounding Christy's death bed to put my arms round my wife. My Niece, one of the nurses, quickly held me back and said,

"Uncle don't worry, we will take care of the rest."

Those words hit me like a bomb and I lost my mind.

"The cruel hand of death has snatched my wife away;" I said silently to myself as I broke down.

She did not appear to have gone through pains going home but for me, losing her companionship just six years into her leading me to know God and embrace salvation at the time I did was a terrible pain. I was distraught, and it felt like a part of me had been ripped off. It was sudden, and the pain was deep. The whole episode lasted less than twenty-four hours and it was all over!

"What a way for a glorious union to end," my mind quivered. God had in His all-knowing called His daughter home and there was nothing else I, not even the doctor or anyone else, could do about it but to submit to His will – and we did.

Isedua and her husband, Ese had won the American Visa Lottery prior to the transition of her mother, Christiana and a few months after the funeral ceremonies they both travelled to join her sister Obehiaye in the United States of America in 2003.

GRIEVING THE LOSS OF A LOVED ONE

Since we got married in 1968, Christiana and I had never lived apart except for the nine months I left her and Godfrey in Lagos after my retirement in 1992. My initial fear was how I could live on without Christiana, my best friend, my confidant. I decided to quickly inform all our kids.

"How will they take the sad news that their mother has passed away only one day after they knew she became sick?" I almost went to pieces.

"Who will now live with me in our home, isolated from the rest of the village, where we both had lived together since relocating to Irrua from Lagos, Nigeria?"

My head was processing too many questions at the same time, to which I was too confused to provide answers.

Totally oblivious that Godfrey was standing by my side in the hospital while I stared at the lifeless body of his mother, I instinctively asked aloud,

"God! what did I do wrong?"

And as if he was God, Godfrey replied, clinging to me, "Daddy, you did not do anything wrong."

Godfrey is our youngest son and although he was in his early twenties and already in the university, ideally, he should have been the last of our kids to be informed of what just happened, but there he was, the only child around me - through it all! That feeling increased my pain as I tried hard to betray my anguish.

As I stood there in the hospital environment, I battled to fight back tears and was overcome by the thought of how I could go home alone when I came to the hospital with my wife. I knew that I wasn't leaving her in a hospital ward for treatment - she just slipped through my fingers – dead and gone without saying a proper goodbye to me, to her kids and her only grandchild, Ehimare whom she had loved so much. During all these, when we arrived home my worry was about Godfrey and I asked him,

"how are you taking it, son?"

"Daddy," he said, "my greatest regret is that she will not see me graduate".

I was moved with compassion and wished I could change that; but I knew I couldn't. I consoled him even as I fought back tears with "don't worry son, your siblings and I will always be there for you." I assured him. But I knew nobody could fill that void permanently left by his mother.

ACKNOWLEDGING A KIND GESTURE.
It is worthy of mention here that for the next few days following the death of my wife, without any prompting, the Chief Medical Director of Irrua Specialist Teaching Hospital was kind enough to send a doctor to my house every morning to check my blood pressure and general wellbeing. That was a very thoughtful gesture that I could not forget in a hurry.

The next few days were tough for me and I knew that the circumstances made me sometimes behave like a child when the weakness of man took over my sense of reasoning. Even when I knew that Christiana was no more, I continually had a yearning to find her in every room that I entered in our home if only to ask her, stupidly perhaps, "why did you have to leave us"!

Why did you not give me the chance of a few days or weeks to fight for your life?"

Yes, I knew I could never have won against the Will of God, even if she gave me months, but I would have wished for it to last for a little while to prepare my mind for what turned out to be the eventual devastating outcome. But could you blame me? Here was a woman we lived together for over thirty-four years and not once did we have cause to wash our "dirty linen" in public –

not even any member of our two families had cause to settle any quarrel between us; and she just left!

My emotions ran wild and then went to Christiana's only grandson, Ehimare, (meaning God's will), whom we were raising together. He was just over two years old and the source of our joy at a time all our own kids had grown and left home. Talking to no one in particular, and in real deep pain and soliloquy, I asked,

"Lord, what should I now do with Ehimare, and who will help me care for him?"

When later I had time to be all by myself, God helped me to answer that one question.

"I'll keep Ehimare, no matter what! God knows why Christiana had to go now." I said to myself.

A tough decision it was to raise a two years old baby alone without a wife, and I was still working. I had made the decision but how I would accomplish it remained a mirage. All I knew was that he would be my only solace and I felt I could not entrust him to any other woman who might not care for him as I would like to.

That was how much Christiana and I were attached to Ehimare. I just prayed to God to give me the Grace and all I would ever need to raise him –and faithful God - He did. From then on, I took Ehimare with me to almost everywhere I went, even sometimes to work if for any reason he did not go to the catholic kindergarten we took him to each day before his grandmother passed away. My kids, Gillian and Godfrey, were immensely helpful coming around time and again to check on us. Godfrey, who was in the University Campus had to eventually relocate back to the house from where he drove to school each day because of Ehimare. Fortunately, Ehimare was such a quiet child who cried only when he was hungry, feeling sleepy or hurt and once he got attention, he could play alone with his toys for hours. I believed that it was the Grace of God that he was also hardly ever sick, thus giving me no reasons to regret the decision to keep him.

THE MYSTERIOUS WAYS OF GOD.

Often, when God is working out certain plans in our lives, we sometimes fail to appreciate them because being mortals, we cannot see beyond the present. At the time Ehimare was about to be born, his father, George, our second son, was still taking a diploma course at the University of Lagos. My wife and I were all over him, so to speak, for what we called 'indiscretion' on his part that resulted to the boy's birth because George was still in school. That was why Christiana and I were the ones raising his baby after he was born. Ikwor, Ehimare's mother was a house help living with my eldest daughter Gladys when she met my son, George and became pregnant for him. Because my daughter, her guardian, was also pregnant at the same time, we brought the girl to live with us in Irrua, Edo State, Nigeria, where she gave birth to Ehimare. Gladys on the other hand had earlier given birth to a set of twins and the young girl offered to go and help her after weaning her own baby. She agreed to leave Ehimare with us.

It is remarkable that at the time Christiana passed away suddenly, the respectable traditional funeral she was consequently accorded stemmed from the fact that she had become a grandmother because of the birth of Ehimare. Without what we gave the toga of 'indiscretion' on the part of his father George, my late wife Christiana might not yet have become a grandmother at the time of her passing. That could only have been God at work while we mere mortals blamed the vessels He used.

God has been faithful; at the time I traveled to the United States, in 2009, Ehimare was already nine years old and I left him in the care of his biological father, George hoping to return to Nigeria in a matter of months. That was not to be for many reasons. He is a teenager now and in secondary school, but I still live with the pain that he did not get to know his grandma to appreciate how much she had loved him. I still miss his company a whole lot.

RESISTING PRESSURE TO RE-MARRY

Losing a loved one in such sudden circumstances could be devastating. When your loved one dies after a period of declining health, it gives you time to condition your mind for any eventuality, but not so in my case. My wife's death came as suddenly as did whatever led to it. For weeks after the event, I just went blank and could hardly believe what just hit me. It was, therefore, heart breaking for me when only a few months after my wife was called to Glory, I got promptings from some people close to me to consider taking another wife. I guessed they meant well, but I considered it uncharitable so soon after losing a vital part of me to so suggest. The wound in my heart had not even started to heal, and I found myself asking, "am I being advised to re-marry?" "What would be the driving force at my age - sixty-six years! – to have children? No, we already had eight and I desired no more!" I told myself.

I knew death had ended the marriage between Christiana and I, and the law, the custom and the church allowed me to re-marry.

"But if God permitted the one woman He chose for me to leave in the circumstances Christiana did, after thirty-four years of living together, leaving me with eight children and her only grandson we were raising together, then that is it, I am done with marriage." I resolved.

I did not have any double mind about that; I did not believe that God called Christiana home because he wanted me to "try" another woman.

"No, there can't be another woman out there for me and I do not believe there is any that can take her place in my heart." I reassured myself.

It's been sixteen years now since Christiana left and God has continued to strengthen me in my resolve. I hope one day to be reunited with my Christiana, my beloved wife and best friend for over thirty-four years. She went home peacefully to be with The Lord she had served so faithfully.

To this day, Christiana still lives in my heart, and always will. I still miss her companionship because she was unique in many ways. What more can I say? In the words of Jim Reeves,

'I know I'll never find another you.'

THE UNEXPECTED DEATH OF MY SON

I was in the middle of writing this book when my eldest son, Gregory, who had battled with cancer of the stomach for some months finally gave in to the scourge, and he joined his late mother in heaven. My son and I had both discussed about this book and he assured me he would contribute to its publishing. Alas! Not anymore. Below is my Tribute to the memory of my late son, Gregory.

"TRIBUTE TO MY BELOVED SON LATE GREGORY OMOHOMION EIGBOBO

The time was thirty-five minutes past six o'clock on a cold morning of October 16, 2017. My daughter, Obehiaye showed up in my room.

"Good morning Daddy, this one that you are still sleeping

now, are you ok?" She asked, acting as if she was full of life and all was well.

"Good morning darling," I replied.

"I did not sleep early last night because I was waiting to speak with Greg in Nigeria before going to bed." I told her.

As I struggled to rise from my bed, I noticed that my son-in-law, Shola, was following his wife behind. He accosted me by the door as I tried to go use the restroom.

Such scenario usually happened in the past only if something ominous had either occurred or was about to occur. I quickly adjusted myself and sat back on my bed, my instincts hardly going to my eldest son Gregory who had been sick. Shola who, by the way is a Pastor, blocking my way started,

"the bible tells us that in all things we must give thanks to God....."

He had hardly finished that bible quotation when I looked him and his wife Obehiaye straight in the eyes curiously. I immediately knew that something sinister had happened and they were trying hard to find the right words to break the sad news to me; but with the wisdom of an elder, I made it easier for them.

"Gregory, my son has gone, right?" I asked.

Then there was dead silence in the room as they looked at themselves. Obehi, who had previously tried hard to conceal her anguish came close and hugged me passionately. "Am so sorry dad" she said.

That alone told the entire story and provided the answer I

had sought.

"Daddy," Shola continued, "we were informed well after mid-night, but we decided to wait till this morning to allow you sleep. We are so sorry dad."

Then I sat back speechless for a little while and all I could say was, "God, I thank you." And I said to Shola and Obehi,

"I woke up last night at about three o'clock a.m. and could no longer go back to sleep, try as I did. I had tossed from side to side on my bed restless up to the time you both came to my room."

Presumably, that was about the exact time my spirit was telling me that my son's soul was leaving his body to return to his maker peacefully. Oh, Greg! He fought to the end.

Earlier that night I had called my daughter, Omonigho (Greg's immediate younger sister) in Nigeria just after mid-night but I could not speak with Gregory on the phone. She had told me that her brother was doing okay and that he could not speak with me because he was asleep. I was pained because I had not spoken with him directly for a few days. Little did I know that Greg. had been rushed to a hospital and was fighting life's final battle alone as I spoke on the telephone with his sister, Omonigho! He was later to transit to Glory a few hours after my conversation with his sister! Rather than call me back to break the sad news, Omonigho in her wisdom called her sister Obehi and her husband Shola instead *that night to tell them, "we just lost him!"*

My son Gregory had battled with ulcer for many years. He was on a deliberate weight loss program, he had told me, and when the fatal cancer of the stomach afflicted him, an unexplained weight loss resulted, but he could not tell the difference between that and his deliberate weight loss effort for many months. That obviated the need for early diagnosis and treatment. When the process eventually commenced unnecessary delays, occasioned by the lack of adequate health care facilities, did not help matters; release of laboratory test results took too long as time flew by.

The entire process was slow, and I feared time was running out on us. Greg was eventually diagnosed with cancer and had a procedure to stop the spread. I was happy when the procedure was said to be successful. Weeks passed after he did, but he was not gaining any weight and he was still losing blood; His sister Obehi and I then thought about other options but at the time, we found out that it had become apparent that in the condition he was, he could no longer withstand a long-distance flight anymore unless the bleeding could be stopped. That did not happen. The thought of it broke my heart, and we then relied only on God's miracle to save my son.

How I wish we knew early enough exactly what was happening to Greg. At the end, we lost him; I am badly pained. My son had fought the good fight and he had finished the race. Greg, as I fondly called him, was a son who could "unlock" my heart, who understood whatever I needed him to do even at the snap of two fingers. If losing a good wife (his late mother) several years earlier was devastating for me, losing him now, a trusted son whose responsibility it would have been to lead his siblings to bury me after my earthly life, was like the whole of my world turning upside down! Only the Almighty God can comfort me now! If it is His will that Greg's earthly life should end at noon, so be it. He is our creator and we cannot question His will.

Gregory would have turned forty-eight years of age on November 6, 2017 when he transited to Glory and in addition to me, he has left behind his amiable wife Carol and three kids, numerous brothers & sisters, and a host of other family relations and friends. His remains are being committed to mother earth today October 20, 2017 in my home town, Irrua.

My son Greg was a unifying factor everywhere he found himself, most of all in our family circle and that of his numerous friends. My entire family will miss him, and I pray that God in His infinite mercy will receive his gentle soul and forgive him all his sins. He will live forever in my heart because he was special in many ways. Adieu my beloved son until we meet at the feet of Jesus to part no more. Adieu, Adieu, Adieu. October 20, 2017."

I have continued to mourn my wife Christiana and now my son, Gregory and do not know if I can ever stop!

RESILIENCE WITH GOD'S HELP – A GRANDFATHER'S PRAYER.

Lord, we look at our family and realize that change is all around us. Our children are adults now. Our Grandchildren are getting taller than we are. We need a course, Lord, on how to adjust and recover from all the changes around us! Create resilience in us in order that we can gracefully meet the challenges of these days. Help us to realize that we are changing as well. It is so easy to treat family members as we did twenty years ago. The love is still there, but our behaviors sometimes need an overhaul. We pray today that our children and grandchildren have resilience also, as they attempt to deal more appropriately with their aging parents. Thank you, Lord, for your resilience as you continue to love and forgive all of us. Amen.

CHAPTER 8

A Test of Faith – My Journey to Salvation

Up until I met Christiana, fell in love with her and we got married, I was only a nominal Christian. I knew about God but did not have intimate relationship with Him, and because I did not come from a strong Christian religious background, I went to church then only at Christmas and Easter; I had not even been baptized!

The closest I ever got to take the first step of faith was sometime around 1956 when a popular American Evangelist, now late, held a mammoth evangelistic crusade at the Race Course in Lagos, Nigeria. It attracted hundreds of thousands Christian adherents. I was almost twenty years old then and was one of a huge crowd of listeners that answered an alter call that night, my first ever, where I 'ignorantly' professed to give my life to Christ. Follow-up committees were set up after the crusade, but I guess my faith then was at the lowest ebb and I could not sustain the momentum because I was not even going to any church; so, I went back into my shell and remained there until I met Christy.

Conversely, Christiana had a strong Christian religious background and was raised a Roman Catholic. She attended church regularly all the while we lived in Lagos and when God started to bless us with kids, she showed each of them the way to the church and to have a relationship with God early. All our kids received infant baptism and early confirmation with my active moral and financial support notwithstanding the fact that I was still "sitting on the fence", so to speak.

Ironically, from 1971, even when by God's Grace we acquired the family's first car, because my wife had not yet learned to drive, I still drove her and the kids to church every Sunday morning and returned to the house to sit down, do nothing until it was time for mass to end; then I would drive back to bring them home. In other words, I still resisted going to church. That went on in Lagos and even when we returned to our home town, Irrua, in Edo State of Nigeria.

Within the confines of our home, however, Christiana ceaselessly maintained gentle pressure on me to change my reluctant attitude towards attending Sunday masses with my family, and truly accept Christ as my Lord and savior. To be honest, I was not averse to serving God properly but was just an irreligious person then who had not yet taken a definite position. The message Christiana was passing on had reached my head but not yet my heart. For twenty-eight years after our marriage I struggled with the idea until one day in 1996 the Holy Spirit gripped my heart and pulled me down on God's side of the fence; the devil was put to shame when I took the first step towards putting the past behind me.

What intrigued me was my wife's demeanor through it all. She never once attempted to force the issue and she showed no anger or frustration at my recalcitrance all through those twenty-eight years; not even when she knew that her not yet receiving the sacrament of holy matrimony in the catholic church placed limitations on some aspects of her worship. She was a devout Christian who exhibited very rare Christian attributes for which I always respected her then and still do to this day - even in death.

THE TURNING POINT

God's time is the best time, and when He calls no one fails to answer. There was this young Monk and a Priest at Saint Benedict Monastery, Ewu in Esan Central Local Government Area of Edo State. He occasionally came to celebrate mass at Annunciation Catholic Church, Eguare, Irrua, where my wife and our kids worshipped; and he had become a friend of our family.

Christiana had informed the priest of the sixtieth anniversary of my birthday on May 9, 1996 and requested for prayers for our family. I was later to know that the following conversation ensued.

"Fr., my husband will be turning sixty in a few days' time; please pray for our family."

"Sixty years is a milestone, why don't we book a mass for him?" the Priest asked her.

"But my husband has not started to attend church and has not even given his life to Christ yet." Replied Christiana.

"In that case, we will take the mass to him at home; invite a few friends," suggested the priest.

" I will discuss it with my husband." She replied.

I noticed that she was surprised at my excitement when she discussed it with me. We invited a few family friends. The mass was celebrated in our home without either my wife or the priest saying even one word to me about going to church, contrary to my expectation. (I believe that bringing the mass to my home on that day was enough strategy and the priest had no need to preach to me about going to church); and it worked! I felt uncomfortable and wondered if everybody had given up on me. That odd feeling, the fact that I could not receive Holy Communion at a mass celebrated in my own home, and in my honor on my birthday anniversary thoroughly embarrassed me. I felt odd amid our invitees as they received holy communion, and I believe that must have immediately precipitated in me a change of heart.

That was the turning point. I went to bed with that odd feeling and later that same night, I suddenly woke up from what was like a dream. I had a feeling that I was only half asleep and I felt an unusual kind of peace within me. I sat up for a little while and what I felt was like God saying to me, "it's time to go."

But go to where, I did not understand. It was not a dream— 1 guessed at that stage, I had allowed the Holy Spirit to take control of my heart; I did not fight back, and I was wide awake! Inside me I knew something was building up. The transformation was spontaneous. I woke my wife up and, without telling her about my experience, said to her, "I'll go to church with you next

Sunday so that we can have a thanksgiving mass."
Without any comment Christiana turned the other way and slept again. I guessed she did not believe me - who would after twenty-eight years of seemingly fruitless gentle pressure?
"She must really have given up on me," I thought, and that, of course, strengthened my resolve. I was ready to disappoint her for once.
That thought notwithstanding, I was up early on Sunday morning and got dressed for church, in fulfillment of my promise. We drove to church without discussing about my new-found interest. I stayed for mass and as I sat there, my whole being was taken over by expectancy completely oblivious of all worldly things around me. I quietly repented of my sins and prayed to God for forgiveness. I visualized a future of being one with my wife and children in Christ Jesus and felt already forgiven by God instantly.
Almost the whole congregation later accompanied us to the altar during my birthday anniversary thanksgiving. After the mass, most of our family friends gathered around me, asking,
"we trust that this is the beginning and we will continue to see you every Sunday in church?"
"Yes," I assured them.
As we headed back home, twice Christiana looked at me and smiled. I pretended to not notice her, but I could feel the joy in her heart, her countenance was like

someone who just had a dream come true. She tried to hide it, but it was written all over her. The ice was broken, and from that day on, I have tried hard to remain focused on and faithful to Jesus.

Surprisingly, Christiana and I never talked about the events of that fateful night up to the day she was called home. She did not bring up the conversation and I did not want to bring it up but, perhaps, it was enough to know that night changed my whole life. She must have heaved a sigh of relief. I believe salvation is a personal choice and I recognize that God can also use someone else as a vehicle on the journey towards achieving it; Christiana offered herself to be used in my own case.

FINDING THE WAY AND PEACE.

Soon after "finding the way" and building up my faith, at my request, the Priest arranged private Catechism lessons for me which I took very seriously to enable me to prepare to receive my first sacrament - baptism. For a start he told me to recite the apostle's creed; I did without error and that pleased him. A few months later I was put to the full test and I believe he was satisfied.

"I think you are ready to receive the sacrament of baptism." He said to me.

A few weeks later in the presence of Christiana and a small congregation at the Annunciation Catholic church, Irrua, I received the sacrament on one cool evening in 1996 after I had truly accepted Jesus Christ as my Lord and Savior.

Hurrah! I was born again after sixty years of struggle! By the special permission of the Archbishop of the Archdiocese, I also received the sacrament of confirmation on the Sunday after my baptism. On August 10, 1996, Christiana and I were united in holy matrimony. Just as I promised God and the congregation in my brief remarks after the ceremony, I have not looked back ever since both in my marital life and religious life.

That's how I was led to the church and to know God intimately through the untiring efforts of a woman God Himself planted in my life. I had traded my shackles for a glorious song and I was free at last. Christiana was raring to go. Happily, my initial iniquity was no longer there to hold either of us down. To God be the Glory, we were both free to participate fully in all the activities of His church and the Christian world at large. At last Christiana's patience had paid off and I felt a sense of achievement and fulfillment as did my wife. Subsequently, it became only a matter of time before she was elected to the position of President, Catholic Women Organization first at Unit level and later at Parish level, a position she held to the day the Angels came knocking to lead her home.

PROFESSED OBLATES AT BENEDICTINE MONASTERY

In addition to hitting the ground running after uplifting my faith by joining some other apostolate societies in the church, about one year after I finally gave my life to Christ, Christiana and I became regular visitors to the Benedictine Monastery close to us. We later formed part of the pioneer oblates team of the Order of St. Benedict (OOSB), an apostolate society in the Catholic Church whose members assist Monks in propagating the tenets of monastic life to lay faithful. We remained 'Professed Oblates' of Saint Benedict until I said goodbye to Christiana in 2002.

In 2006, the young Priest, (Dr.) and Monk as he had then become, was again the officiating priest at my seventieth birthday anniversary mass at my request.

"I accepted the invitation to celebrate this mass today at the birthday anniversary of Sir. Eigbobo because I have a story to tell." Those were his words at the commencement of his homily to the congregation. He went on to recount not only my faith journey to salvation but also the great strides he said he was proud that I had taken within the ten years of my Christian life which culminated to my rise to a position of First Vice District Commander in the Ancient and Noble Order of Knights & Ladies Auxiliary of Saint John International (KSJI) in the Catholic Church. He described the modest achievements as 'remarkable'; for me, that was humbling.

LAUDABLE ACHIEVEMENTS OF CHRISTIANA.

To Christiana's credit, prior to my receiving the sacrament of baptism, she had also earlier led my ninety years old mother, Theresa, who hitherto had never been to church, to know God intimately. She eventually received the sacraments of baptism and confirmation also in 1996 - ten years before my late mother was called home in 2006 at the ripe age of one hundred years! That singular conversion got her saved and qualified her for the proper Christian funeral which the church and the family deservedly accorded her. I had no doubt in my mind that she had repented and that even God might have forgiven her whatever sins she might have committed while on earth.

ERECTING THE GROTTO.

When Christiana and I moved back to Irrua in 1992, she noticed that as big and old as the Annunciation Catholic Church, Eguare, Irrua was, no Grotto was erected in honor of our Mother Mary. As one of her laudable achievements as President of Catholic Women Organization, Annunciation Catholic parish, Irrua, she conceived the idea of one being erected at the parish main church as part of her legacy. She sold the idea to the parish Administrator and, as President of Catholic

Women Organization, she spearheaded the efforts to raise money from several sources and the project was commenced. As if there was a force pushing her, she worked tirelessly, throwing everything into the effort to complete the erection of the Grotto.

Unfortunately, it was not the will of God that she would be the one to complete its erection, and she could therefore not see it to fruition due to paucity of funds before her home call. I knew that she was very passionate about erecting the Grotto. In my tribute to Christiana at the funeral mass celebrated to honor her, I wrote inter alia in the funeral program: -

"If she will have any regrets at all wherever she may be, it is her inability to see to fruition the completion of The Grotto in honor of our Mother Mary, a project which she held very close to her heart."

The officiating priest at the funeral mass amplified those words during his homily. He had specifically flown in all the way from the United States of America, where he was undertaking his doctorate, to celebrate the funeral mass.

To God be the glory, that message resonated in the hearts of many in the congregation, particularly members of the Ancient and Noble Order of Knights & Ladies Auxiliary of Saint John International (KSJI) who represented various Local commanderies within the Lagos Grand Commandery. A total cash donation and pledges of over two hundred and fifty thousand naira was raised on the spot specifically for that purpose at the funeral mass. It was heartwarming for me to know that the amount was sufficient to complete the project which to date adorns the premises of the Annunciation Catholic Church, Eguare- Irrua in Nigeria.

WINNING SOULS FOR GOD'S KINGDOM

Souls can be won for God's Kingdom through various ways and means. One of my cousins and friend was in the church with his wife on the day Christiana and I were joined together in holy matrimony. He walked up to me after the mass, looked me in the eye and said to me, "congratulations cousin, but m- e- n, you have put me under pressure. I know from now on my wife won't let me rest."

"Yes, I know, but I think it will be worth all the trouble." I admonished him.

Like me, he had also been married for many years to a devout Christian raised in the catholic faith and, his wife, like mine, was attending church alone because her husband, like me, was obstinate. Unlike me, however, who did not receive baptism until after my sixtieth birthday, I believe my cousin got baptized as a teenager, possibly because he attended a catholic secondary school. Again, like me, he was only a nominal Christian and might possibly have gone back to the world and forgotten all about church as soon as he was through with his secondary school education.

I did not know what went on within the confines of their own home but, after about one year or so, my cousin had renewed his baptismal vow. Like me, he also led his wife to the altar and they were joined together in holy matrimony. I believe like me, he has also not looked back ever since. That's one way a soul was won back into God's Kingdom more by action than preaching!

It's never too late to accept Jesus Christ as our Lord and Savior. The examples of my mother and I are typical. Let us look back over our experiences along life's journey; we might have had regrets about certain choices we made but we should not allow them to weigh us down and stand between us and the salvation we so much desire. Jesus is always calling us to turn away from our iniquities and come to Him. The bible tells us that He is the only way. Whenever you wake up is your own morning, and whatever it was that had held you down, no matter for how long, remember, that was then, and - this is now! All you need is to take the first step, if you have not done so already, and with the help of the Holy Spirit, you will conquer the devil.

During her earthly life, with the help of God, Christiana and I had tried hard to make positive impact on the lives of all those who had associated with us to the best of our ability. In pursuance of that objective, between 1996 and until Christiana was called home in 2002 after a brief illness, we had both actively participated in various apostolate societies in the church to the glory of God viz:

1. Membership of Sacred Heart of Jesus & Immaculate Heart of Mary Annunciation Catholic Church, Eguare-Irrua.
2. Pioneer membership of the Professed Oblates of Saint Benedict, Benedictine Monastery, Ewu, (OOSB).
3. Pioneer initiates of the Ancient & Noble Order of the Knights & Ladies Aux. of Saint John International (KSJI).

I was also a patron to Altar Boys & Girls, ACC Eguare Unit, Irrua and Patron, Adorers at ACC Eguare Unit, Irrua.

KNIGHTS AND LADIES AUX. OF ST. JOHN INTERNATIONAL (KSJI).

Christiana and I were initiated into the Ancient and Noble Order of Knights & Ladies Auxiliary of Saint John International on June 1, 2002 and together with the other sixteen couples also initiated, we were anxiously awaiting the inauguration of our new Uromi Commandery. As if God had waited to use Christiana as the vehicle to save me and my mother from condemnation, He called her home peacefully barely five months after our initiation into the Knights & Ladies Aux. of Saint John International. (KSJI). One month after Christiana's funeral mass on 21st November, 2002, I was unanimously elected as the pioneer Worthy President of the new commandery 556, Uromi in December 2002 for a first term of three years.

With the help of God's Grace, I led a seventeen-member pioneer Knights and sixteen Ladies Aux. to build the commandery to a total of one-hundred-member team within three years. Under my leadership, discussion was initiated which was later to bring about the birth of a new commandery at Ekpoma in Esan West Local Government Area of Edo State, Nigeria, mothered by commandery 556, Uromi.

VOLUNTARY WITHDRAWAL FROM RE-ELECTION

Elections were generally fixed for the third Saturday of November in Knight of St. John International. After my first term, the date for the next election was fixed for November 19, 2005. That date coincided with the wedding day of Gregory, my eldest son, in Lagos which I could not afford to miss. I voluntarily withdrew from seeking re-election since, according to the rules, I had to be physically present to be nominated, vote and be voted for. In any event, I had reasoned that the availability of possible fresh ideas from a successor Worthy President could have the effect of continuing the development of the young commandery and the overall Noble Order of Knights & Ladies Aux. of Saint John International (KSJI) to the glory of God. However, it seemed as if God was saying to me, "your leadership qualities are still needed in the Order" because just two months after, in January 2006, I got elected, without seeking, to the higher rank of 1ˢᵗ Vice District Commander, District Eleven comprising all the local commanderies within Edo and Delta States under the Lagos Grand Commandery for a term of three years.

The story of my faith journey cannot be complete without me returning to God the glory for the divine inspiration, through His servants, the Priest, and the love of my life, Christiana, for me to be saved and get the opportunity to serve Him faithfully. May Christiana's gentle soul continue to rest in the bosom of The Lord, and may God continue to strengthen His Priest as he serves in His vineyard.

CHAPTER 9

SOCIAL & SPORTING ACTIVITIES

I had planned a regimented social and sporting life for myself as a young adult to provide room for recreation amid a busy schedule even in my struggling years. All work and no play, they say, makes Jack a dull boy; so, I found time to relax amid all my serious struggles.

Ballroom dancing was very popular in my time and I had spent eighteen months learning basic, intermediate and advanced ballroom dancing skills side by side with focusing on my secretarial studies. I was a prolific ballroom dancer and enjoyed the art so very much. I won a few dancing competitions in and outside of Lagos including one All Lagos ballroom dancing schools' competition in the early sixties. I also enjoyed going to parties and picnics where dancing skills could be exhibited. I was an active member of the popular Lagos Arcade, and Obalende Police Barracks Ballroom Dancing Schools in Lagos between 1956 and 1966.

Suddenly, virtually all the ballroom dancing schools in Lagos, Nigeria were involuntarily forced to shut down in 1966 when it became no longer safe to move about freely once it was dark because of the overzealous behavior of some members of a section of the Nigerian military personnel after the second military coup in Nigeria in July of that year. Many of the military personnel took advantage of the coup to continually step out of the barracks to unduly intimidate members of the civilian population ostensibly to simply amplify the fact that the military was then in power. All the dancing schools have remained non-functional even when the country returned to democratic rule.

FORMATION OF "THE ELEPHANT BOYS" FOOTBALL CLUB

Unable to advance my interest in playing football (soccer) due mainly to parental restrictions as a youngster, I refused to allow my interest in it to die. When I was employed in Bank of West Africa Limited, I joined some other members of staff to form what is now known as First Bank Football Club which we christened "The Elephant Boys" in Lagos in the mid-sixties. Roberts, a Briton was the pioneer chairman of the club and I was privileged to serve as the pioneer General Secretary for the first seven years after its formation.

I eventually became a member of the then Lagos Amateur Football Association (LAFA) through the instrumentality of the football team when it was registered for the Lagos League Division three competition. The team progressively merited promotions from Division three to two, and later to Division One of the Lagos Amateur Football Association Leagues. The team had continued to do well up to the time I retired in 1992. I understand it's now competing in the current Nigerian National Soccer League.

I am particularly proud to know that the football club is still in existence and growing. When it was first formed, the then management of the Bank neither showed interest nor recognized its existence, even after we informed the Bank Management that running a football club in the bank's name was cheap advertisement for the bank. At some point, to ensure that the club was not allowed to die, a few of us sometimes contributed our personal money to transport players to practice and match venues simply for the love of the game. It was not until the team started to win matches and was to be registered with the Lagos Amateur Football Association, Division three league competition that the bank management began to show interest in and provide funds to run its affairs. Against all entreaties, but because of the distance, I voluntarily relinquished the position of General Secretary of the club to allow room for effective co-ordination of activities when I was transferred to Stationery & Supplies department of the bank and I needed to move from Lagos Island to Apapa also in Lagos.

PHOTO SPEAK

Winning a Ballroom Dancing

Two Daughters Wedding

Receiving Certificate of honour

Gilbert & Christy Eigbobo

Self as First Vice District CDR

Gilbert as Worthy President of Commandery 556 Uromi

PHOTO SPEAK

Gilbert & Christy Eigbobo

Professed Oblates of St. Bernedict at Ewu Monastry

First Kids Arrive

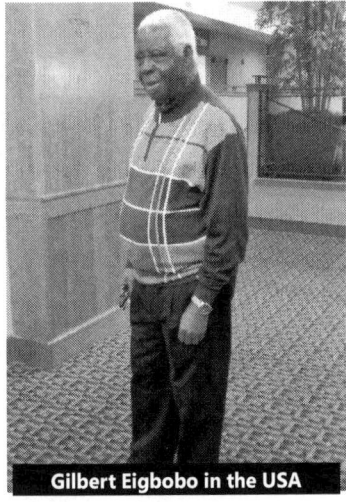
Gilbert Eigbobo in the USA

CONCLUSION:

I enjoyed playing lawn and table tennis games as hobbies and was a member of the popular Lagos Country Club, Ikeja, Lagos, up until I relocated from Lagos after retiring from the services of First Bank in 1992.

I was a Founding member of Irrua Welfare Association, Lagos, my town's union, and served as President for several years until I relocated to Irrua in 1992.

I was presented with a Certificate of Honor by His Royal Highness the Traditional Ruler of my Town for "Outstanding contribution to the welfare and development of the Kingdom and people".

I was a Founding member of Okaijesan Club of Irrua and served as Treasurer. I was also chairman, organizing committee of its development fund raising program which took Irrua by storm and brought a well-known philanthropist, now late, from Lagos to Irrua live in 1987 as chief launcher.

I was a Founding member of Idumebo Family Union and served as General Secretary for many years prior to returning to Irrua in 1992. I was a Founding member of Eigbobo Descendants Family Association. I was also a Patron to: Summit Club of Nigeria, Irrua.

Aikore Club of Irrua, and Esan '83 Club in Lagos.

CHAPTER 10

THE CHARACTERISTICS OF AGING PROCESS.

Growing old is not by choice; it is a process and not an event or even an idea. Like retirement, it will gradually crawl along if you live long enough. The line dividing middle age and old age is very thin and invisible. Old age sets in gradually; no one escapes it unless by early death, and there is no specific time for designating anyone as old.

Aging therefore begins to set in from the moment you are no longer able to do some of the things you once did, even when you feel healthy and there has been no change in your daily activities. That is the right time to begin to adjust to the reality of your new circumstances. No scientific inventions have succeeded to slow down, stop, or reverse human aging. Some might have succeeded to remove the wrinkles and eye bags we develop along the way and seemingly make us look younger again, but none has ever stopped aging irrespective of race, stature or color. We must age no matter the scientific antics!

Before I turned seventy years of age way back in Nigeria, I could jog half of the three kilometers distance I used to exercise each morning before going to my office without feeling tired. Even when I first visited Garland, Texas in 2007, one year after my seventieth birthday, I was still able to run after my grandkids, Daniel and David, up and down the stair way. I even occasionally took them to Audubon Park in Garland for soccer practice for about one hour, and still walked the distance back to the house without feeling fatigued.

Daniel and David are now entering their teenage years and when I took them out to the lawn tennis court a few years back, the kids hit the ball so hard and fast that I found out that I could no longer return their balls unless the ones that came directly to me or close to wherever I positioned myself at the tennis court. That implied that while their bones had grown stronger as they look forward to their teenage years, my own, and my reflexes had grown weaker as I became older. That was my first indication that I had turned one more bend and was aging.

Lately, I found out that I could only walk the whole distance of my daily exercise route – without jogging any longer. My doctors tell me it's ok to walk; and it would have been foolhardy to do otherwise because I no longer had the stamina. I discovered also that sometimes, it was becoming difficult to climb the stairway without the aid of the banister to maintain a balance; and yet, I had not stopped exercising! I have had to ask myself,

"at what point did all the energy and reflex leave me?" The answer I got was "progressively!"

Other than early death, I am yet to know of anything, anything at all that stops aging; I have not met any person who continued to gain in strength, stamina, agility and reflex as he or she grew from adulthood to old age. Aging therefore, is a slowing down process that causes our muscles to gradually grow stiff and lose strength; in other words, as we get older our strength decreases. Our ability to remember things begin to decline, even our vision and hearing become noticeably impaired through normal aging process which cannot be prevented or stopped by artificial manipulations.

Parents and Grandparents look old and ancient to young children at their middle and old age. Conversely, at old age, most grandparents look at their children and Grandchildren as always young. Yet children want to grow up faster and are always pushing their young age up. Ask a child how old he or she is, and the answer will always end with "and-a-half," or "almost;" never "I was." A ten-year-old can't wait to be twelve. The twelve-year-old wants to be a teenager. The teenage child wants to be old enough to get married. Couples are waiting to give their daughters away in marriage, so they can become Grandparents. Ironically, when they become Grandparents, they begin to complain about their old age. Irrespective of who we are, there is nothing that can halt aging process and whether we like it or not, the longer we live the more age-related burdens and disabilities will become our companions.

AGING GRACEFULLY.

I was going through security check-in to board a flight from Seattle airport to Dallas Fort Worth airport in 2013 and a young airport official said to me, "remove your shoes and your belt sir," as is normal.

"I am a senior." I said to him as he focused on me. Sounding somewhat sarcastic he looked at me and asked, "how old are you?" "Seventy-seven years," I replied. "You sure don't look it sir," he said - now smiling.

"But that's the truth." I assured him and asked, "need to see proof?"

Then with his two hands clenched, still smiling he said, " go ahead sir, I believe you, but I wish I can look like you in my seventies!" I smiled at him and replied, "thanks, bless you".

Even now that I am over eighty-one years old, time and again, in recent times, I have been told often enough something like,

"wao! You don't look eighty;" or "you look ten years (and some even say) twenty years younger."

I just smile and say, "thank you." But deep inside me I know what age I feel; a feeling which is not because of ill-health but is brought about by the inevitable aging process. Nowadays, I sometimes wake up in the morning only to feel pains which I did not go to bed with the night before; they also gradually go away without any treatment; that can be an interesting aspect of aging.

Up to now, one of my Primary healthcare provider's front desk staff often humorously asks me each time I visit on appointment;

"Young man," she would say, "what can we do for you

today?" and we both laugh over it. One day, I asked her,
"Why do you always call me young man? I am over eighty!" I reminded her.

"yes, I know, but because you don't look it!" she replied humorously.

The longer we live the older we inevitably become. Whether we look our age or not, nobody can cheat nature.

I used to have a knack for remembering the birthdays of all my eight kids and I never forgot to call every single one of them on telephone from wherever I was. I wanted to say a happy birthday to my daughter, Isy one day late recently but did not get an answer to my phone call; then I sent a 'Happy Birthday' text to her phone. That was the first time I had ever been late to call her in the over forty years of her life. I apologized and said to her inter-alia,

"Isy, *sorry, daddy has started to forget some things little by little. I love you. Happy birthday"*.

"*Oh, no problem at all daddy, I think you have earned the right to forget some little things."* She said in her reply. "*Nothing replaces your blessings. Thank you, daddy, I Love u too."* I felt tickled.

As I said somewhere else in this book, in all my over eighty-one years, I had never been admitted in any hospital for a whole day for any treatment. In other words, I'd never fallen so seriously sick as to trigger any anxiety, such as "can he pull through?"

Yet, the inevitable changes in my activities had become

apparent, even if they didn't show in my appearance. All these had been enough whispers to my ears that I was aging notwithstanding all the flatter about looking younger than my age. Despite all that aging tells us daily with the changes in our activities, we should have nothing to fear because aging is a gift from God and, for believers, it is a win-win situation. If we live to it before we die, we win, and if we die before reaching old age, we still win. All we need is to do right by our creator while we are alive, and I am confident that He will not let us fall even if we stumble.

After receiving the sacrament of baptism and confirmation at age ninety, my mom lived another ten years before she passed away at the age of one hundred years. I am sure that some unbelievers would think she had waited too long to repent of her sins, but I believe God in His infinite mercy gave her ten more years to work on whatever might not have been right in her ninety years of seeming darkness on earth. I believe too she received God's forgiveness before she was called home. Her own mother had earlier lived to be one hundred and ten years. I watched them both age gracefully without any complicated age-related illness up to the time each of them went home, and they both did peacefully.

I was very close to my grandma and she was also very fond of me, but I did not live with her. When she was growing old, (she had always been old to me as a child anyway,) I remember that each time I visited, she took me either to the farm or behind her house and, along the way, she took pains to show me her economic trees which were part of her assets and she told me to clear the bushes around them. She also told me who of her survivors would own what after her death. I realized after she passed away that was her way of writing her will. Without expressly saying so to me, in the event of conflicts among her children as to who inherited what, she expected that I, coming from outside of her immediate family, could be the "tie breaker." I believed there must have been someone else she similarly showed those assets to. Luckily, no such conflicts arose after her home call.

Some of us age gracefully; no easily discernible wrinkles, no serious inhibitive aches and pains. Others go through it sickly, due to all sorts of complicated health issues, and some others even end up on wheel chair. Howsoever you end up will depend on your life style while you were younger. Wherever you fit in, old age is not to be despised because it is about the only thing that comes to us without our own effort. It is God's gift to only some of His children and if you are lucky to be one of the beneficiaries, savor it, and always remember this prayer:

When I am old and grey, do not forsake me my God till I declare Your power to the next generation. (psalm 71: 18)

PLANNING FOR THE FUTURE.

For all humans, earthly life is transient and physical death is an
inevitable end unless you are lucky to still be here when Jesus Christ returns. Except perhaps in our childhood days when we were not yet conscious of our being, we all make plans at every stage of our lives and must also diligently extend that to the latter years of earthly life. As teenagers and young adults, we make plans for good education; as adults, we dream of and make plans for good jobs, happy families, and even big businesses. Because no one wants to dwell on death, only a few, if any, want to touch the issue of planning for it even with a long pole!

That notwithstanding, at old age, you must not neglect to also plan for your future, including death, which only God knows when it will come. You do not die young because you are a worse sinner than those who live to old age. When we die is simply God's own prerogative and no mortal has yet been able to unravel why some of us die young and others live to old age. It is ironical that only a few people want to discuss death even at old age, yet we know it is inevitable and it will come to us at our creator's appointed time in our lives. Our refusal to discuss it or plan for it does not make it go away.

Part of planning for death is making a will. Again, we do not die early just because we made one, neither do we live to old age because we failed to make any. The exercise is simply to make things easy for the beneficiaries we leave behind. God created us and deliberately kept from us the day and time of our earthly deaths. Anyone who benefits from His gift of old age therefore, must not neglect to plan, otherwise, what happens to all our material acquisitions during our life time which we cannot take along should God call for our souls at a time we failed to make plans?

Growing old presents many challenges. No matter how much you know of the dynamics of your family, making choices for ourselves is difficult, but leaving them to someone else is risky. Unless we take care of them while we are still alive, intruders may step in and make life difficult for the family members we leave behind when we die. We may be leaving behind a plethora of problems, solutions to which are usually protracted and sometimes life threatening these days. If we can plan for our business, then greater pains must be taken to plan for those of our most valued possessions, our spouses and children. There is great wisdom in responsibly caring about the details and following through on them for our own sake and the sake of those we love.

My very close childhood friend suddenly passed away at the age of fifty-two years. He had chaired a society meeting after attending a Sunday mass at his local church, and he helped to put away the chairs. He then drove to a nearby market in the company of his wife to grab a few food stuffs before returning to their house.

He showed no signs of ill health up to that point, but when his wife returned, after staying for about forty minutes inside the market, she met her husband resting his head on the steering wheel of his car, looking exhausted under the burning afternoon sun. She tapped him on the shoulders.

As my friend jerked back to consciousness he said to his wife, "Let's go home."

She didn't think he looked strong enough to drive, but unfortunately, she herself had not yet been licensed to drive.

My friend turned on the car engine, got on the road and soon bumped on the car in front of him. As he tried to get out of his car to see what damage, if any, had been done, he suddenly discovered that his legs were no longer strong enough to support him. He might have slumped there had his wife not quickly helped him back to his seat. She raised an alarm and it took the generosity of a Road Warden on traffic control duty to quickly drive my friend and his wife to a nearby hospital, against the man's request to be driven to his house several miles away. By the time I was informed, and I arrived at the hospital within an hour or two he had gone into a coma. Unfortunately, he did not come out of the coma again up until the time he passed away in the wee hours of the next morning. He was a very active person but because his sudden death was unexpected so to speak, it shocked me greatly.

THE GENESIS OF HIGH BLOOD PRESSURE DIAGNOSIS.

My friend and I were so close that some of our mutual friends, especially at the office where he worked, believed we were brothers. It was after I had given a graveside oration at his funeral, that all of them knew we were just friends!

The death of my friend devastated me and, while at his house accompanied by my wife Christiana, commiserating with his family, Christiana looked at me and said, "papa Greg, your body language shows that you are feeling this tragedy more than you are showing it. Come on, I think you need to see the doctor."

I did that same day, and surprisingly, for the very first time in my life, my blood pressure readings rose above normal. I could not explain why but that explains the level of our friendship. I was immediately placed on control medication and have continued to manage my high blood pressure ever since to this day.

After I overcame the emotional trauma of my friend's passing away, I had promised my wife that I would never again get too close to any friend.

"It is too risky should anything happen to him." I had told her.

But in my lifetime, I have found out that some things are easier said than implemented.

A few years after my friend passed away, it became evident that I was not going to be able to keep my promise to Christiana to live within my own small world. By nature, I had never been an introvert. In other words, I needed companionship, and Luke came handy to fill that void. All I needed was a trusted friend and I tried not to get too close; but as fate was stronger than I, our friendship grew. At some point, my friend and I found out that we were each building a house in the village. We started to travel home together sometimes doing so in one car alternately from Lagos almost at monthly intervals until we completed our projects.

My friend had retired soon after I relocated to my hometown, Irrua, Edo State of Nigeria in 1992. Just about the same time he became obsessed with the idea to also relocate from Lagos, he took ill, had a procedure and later passed away. He was in his early sixties. I was able to cope better with the news of his passing away because, at least, unlike Matt., whose death was sudden, Luke was sick for a longer period and I had the opportunity to travel to Lagos to visit him before his transition.

LEAVING A LEGACY

As parents, our children, and later grandchildren are influenced by our life style - what we say and do - our character. The lives of our children are more directly so influenced but becomes less direct on our grandchildren because they have their own parents with whom they spend more of their time and whose characters tend to shape their lives. We may leave all conceivable material acquisitions when we die but by far the greatest legacy is that innate part of our lives that no one can touch or hold – character!

Our children are different one from another in personality and habits. Therefore, they cannot be influenced equally even with the best of intentions. Two kids may be raised by the same parents under the same circumstances but turn out to be different personalities and characters as they grow older. That phenomenon implies that our influence on our children and all those who are close to us is only a guide in their formative years. Some of them may even reject our effort to guide them. We cannot grudge them that because even though God created us all in His own image, our personalities and characters differ one from another as we grow.

What therefore is the greatest legacy we can leave for our children? To raise them with the fear of God, love and equip them with all that they will need to be able to fit into God's plan for their lives and society; above all, pray for them.

EPILOGUE.

My autobiography would not be complete without me giving God the Glory for my life these past almost eighty-two years, blessing me with such good health that at over eighty-one years, I have never had to sleep on any hospital bed for a whole night because of ill-health thus far. It would be the height of arrogance if I thought that I had carved this good health myself. Yes, God has been faithful. He has kept me, and His Grace has been sufficient for me as I gradually move close to the twilight era of my life.

Therefore Lord, you have allowed my family to grow and expand through these years. As I grow older, help me to realize that aging is the only way to live. Regardless of my years, help me to celebrate your gift of aging each day. May I model the gift of aging as I continue to serve and celebrate life. May my children model what it is to become "empty-nesters" and deal with the challenges of finances, health issues and changes that surround them. May my grandchildren see their future, not through fearful and unfocused ways, but rather through hopeful and encouraging eyes. And may we all grow in our faith in you, even though we may differ on ways to worship, priorities of the Church, and issues of life that can break and bend family togetherness. Through it all Lord, help us to grow, not by attempting to "fix" everything that is wrong with us and them, but rather by growing closer to you, the Lord and giver of growth. Amen.